Advance praise for AMY LANE'S
Crafting Category Romance

"Spectacular. There's gold in this book for everyor̄ ⌐⌐ inner
to master storyteller."

ɔns

ler

"*Crafting Category Romance* is sure to b ....ıy successful authors'
secret weapon in tightening their prose and igniting their readers'
imagination. I know I'll be reading it again and again."

— Carmen Cook
The Sapphire Creek series

"An artful, heart-full guide to the power and potential of category
romance, packed with wisdom and glee and resonant asides that nudge
you toward deeper experimentation. Whether you're drafting your first
book or revising your fifteenth, each of Lane's cheeky, chatty chapters
unpacks the core resources and subtle challenges before you. Delightful."

— Damon Suede
Your A Game, *Activate*, *Verbalize*

"Amy Lane's method works wonders for pantsers as well as plotters—
and everyone in between. Her recipe for success doesn't take away the
creativity in storytelling but gives the author parameters to work within
to craft a romance that readers will devour. I highly recommend this
book for writers of all levels who want to improve their craft and write a
book that's ready for traditional publication."

— R.L. Merrill
The Hollywood Rock n' Romance Trilogy

"*Crafting Category Romance* is the essential guidebook Romance
authors have been waiting for. It is a masterclass in crafting supremely
satisfying romantic arcs. Best of all, it shatters stereotypes about the craft
integrity of category lines and shows what all Romance authors stand to
learn from category romance."

— Kilby Blades
The Modern Love series

CRAFTING CATEGORY ROMANCE

THE ART OF FICTION HAIKU

Amy Lane

CREATIVES

Published by
DSP CREATIVES

5032 Capital Circle SW, Suite 2, PMB# 279, Tallahassee, FL 32305-7886 USA
www.dreamspinnerpress.com

Trade Paperback ISBN: 978-1-64405-807-7
Digital ISBN: 978-1-64405-806-0
Library of Congress Control Number: 2020936844
Trade Paperback published September 2020
v. 1.0

Printed in the United States of America
∞
This paper meets the requirements of
ANSI/NISO Z39.48-1992 (Permanence of Paper).

TABLE OF CONTENTS

DEDICATION

I USUALLY dedicate my books to my family—and Mate and the kids get a nod here because I babbled about this book for*ever* and they deserve some thanks. But this book never would have happened if people like Damon Suede and Elizabeth North and Karen Rose and Tere Michaels and Lynn West and Mary Calmes and Rayna Vause and Brenda Chin hadn't had the solid urge to "talk story" to me at every opportunity.

This book is for every writer who has thought about craft and struggled to perfect it, and has gone on to share what they have learned.

May we continue to talk story until every generation is thrilled at the stories they may tell.

ACKNOWLEDGMENTS

AHERM. DAMON Suede revised this book three times. The first time it was a massive disaster. So, yes, he *did* con me—erm, talk me, erm, convince me to write the damned thing, but he definitely walked the talk when it came to helping me *not* make a complete ass of myself, so he gets an entire paragraph of acknowledgment to his own magnificent person. He's earned it in spades.

But he's not the only one.

Cindy Dees, Anna J. Stewart, and Sue Brown-Moore all gave me quotes and encouragement and also talked story with me and helped this book come to be. Suzanne Brockmann was planning on it—but it turned out I found the perfect interview from a few years ago, so really, all I had to do was wish her safe travels as she navigated the desert. I'm so grateful she was willing. Everyone who helped me with book recommendations, including all of the aforementioned awesomesauce people, and LaQuette, who has been a lovely and true friend, deserves some thanks here.

Brenda Chin edited for me—and we'd only just come to know each other as she edited my fiction through Dreamspinner. She wrote my foreword, she encouraged me, and she told me it didn't suck. And oh boy, did I need to hear that.

Elizabeth North gave me the opportunity with this nonfiction book that I never dreamed of.

So thank you—all of you—for sharing the vast array of your experience and talent. I am in awe of the company I keep—this book couldn't have happened without you.

FOREWORD

I CAN'T remember a time in my life when I wasn't reading everything I could get my hands on. At seven I became a regular at our local library, devouring middle-grade fiction like *Where the Red Fern Grows*, as well as many of the original stories behind my favorite Disney movies—*Peter Pan* by J. M. Barrie, *The Hundred and One Dalmatians* by Dodie Smith, *Bambi* by Felix Salten, *Escape to Witch Mountain* by Alexander Key, and, of course, *The Jungle Book* by Rudyard Kipling. At ten I moved on to my dad's Zane Grey westerns and Frank Yerby's historical epics, as well as my grandmother's Victoria Holt gothics. But one March break when I was twelve, my grandmother gave me Kathleen Woodiwiss's *Ashes in the Wind* to read, and that was it—I was hooked on romance. Throughout my teenage years, I read close to fifteen novels a week— books by Bertrice Small, Jennifer Wilde, Rosemary Rogers, Laurie McBain, and Johanna Lindsey, to name just a few. I couldn't get enough of them.

But it wasn't until I started at Harlequin in 1988 that I read my first category romance novel. Of course, I'd heard of them. But stories featuring meek nurses who fell for rich alpha doctors never really caught my interest. However, once I started working there, I discovered that there was so much more to category romance than I thought. I quickly identified with the strong heroines of Harlequin Temptation, and got my historical fix with Harlequin Historicals, which had just launched earlier that same year. I even learned all about mores and manners of Regency England while working with Marmie Charndoff of Harlequin Regency Romance. Throughout my time at Harlequin, I was lucky enough to work with the editors of almost every romance series coming out of the Toronto office.

I still can't believe it took me all that time to discover one of the greatest treasures in the fiction world—category romance.

While I'll always love reading historicals, category romances give me something altogether different.

They're short, so they don't involve a big time commitment. I can finish a book in an hour or two and get my dose of happiness for the day.

I have a problem putting down a good book (I was in the midnight lineup for the last few *Harry Potter* books. I got the last one at 1:00 a.m. and finished it by 4:00 a.m.), so for me, this instant gratification is important.

I can see myself in the characters. When I worked on Harlequin Temptation and then Harlequin Blaze, I used to say that the heroines got into situations I could have, when I was that age. Only I didn't have the nerve to go for it, and they do. I love living vicariously through characters I like and can identify with.

My favorite authors write a lot of books. In category romance, an author needs to write at least three books a year in order to keep a following (and more is even better). There's nothing worse than having to wait for two years to find out what's going to happen to an interesting character you've just met.

There's a category series for almost everything. Like short and sexy? There are a few series to choose from. Or small-town stories with family values? Suspense? History? Paranormal? You'll find it all in category romance.

A happy ending is a guarantee. You don't have to worry about it. (I'll admit, I read the end of every *Harry Potter* book before starting it. If J.K. Rowling had killed off Harry, as it had been hinted, I wouldn't have read it. Then again, I also stopped reading A Song of Ice and Fire in the third book because I didn't want to see what happened to Robb's wolf. I'll admit it—I'm a bit of a wuss.) That happy ending is everything to category readers. When you've had a bad day, when your life is turning upside down, when nothing looks like it's going right, you can count on a category romance to lift your spirits with a happy ending. That's better than Prozac!

But putting these wonderful tales together isn't easy. In fact, in many cases it's more difficult than writing a single title novel, because the author has fewer words to get the story across, as well as a lot of reader expectations. So what's the secret to writing these shorter stories that mean so much?

That's what you're going to find out in this book. I leave you in the very capable hands of a master storyteller, Amy Lane, who promises to spill some of her secrets in the following pages. I hope you enjoy learning all about the art of Fiction Haiku. I certainly did.

Brenda Chin
Editor

AUTHOR'S NOTE—
AMY'S NOSTALGIA LANE

WHEN I was a kid, reading was not really considered a "valuable" use of my time.

I remember staying with my grandparents and my grandfather getting upset with me because I had my nose in a book—a romance book—60 percent of the time.

"They're all the same," he dismissed. "Boy and girl get together, have sex, whatever. Don't see why you need to be reading them all the time."

"But Grandpa! They're so much more than that!" I told him. But I was fourteen. My vocabulary stalled out at "so much more."

Years later, after a college education and years breaking down the intuitive things I knew about literature for my inner-city high school students, I had better words. I had *trope*, *plot*, *character*, *conflict*, *archetype*, and *theme*. I could explain that romance books operated on the same fictional platform as any other literature, but they came with certain genre expectations that created a smaller, tighter framework they had to work within.

I could explain that category romances adhered to the same plot structure Shakespearean plays did and that the idea of being "surprised" by the outcome of a story was a relatively new rule for pop culture. I could point out that plot—any plot—was designed to do the same things to our body that a pleasant bump of exercise or sex or sugar did, with the added benefit of occupying our minds and increasing our empathy and vocabulary.

I would talk about character, and how just because a character was made to fit into an expected mold didn't mean that character couldn't be a unique individual, much like people we know, and how exciting it was when a character's personality, job, and function in the story actually drove that exciting, comfortable, endorphin-releasing plot. There would be a discussion about tropes and motifs and expectations, and the rush of excitement when those expectations had been met, or exceeded, or turned on their ear.

Conflict would come into the picture, and the different kinds of conflict that can be generated by two strong characters and a little bit of forced contact and the ineffable—but hopefully reproducible—magic of sexual chemistry and conflicting agendas that becomes the friction at the heart of an engaging love story.

There would be some serious adult conversation about how the climax of the story shouldn't be just about sex. It should be about how important it is that two people can forge a life together, and how much hope it gives people.

I know that it gave hope to *me*—both then as an adolescent and now as a woman of age—to see that a happy ending could be forged with hard work and true love. I would want to make that universal.

In short, I'd talk about everything in this book, backed up with empirical evidence and the job knowledge of almost twenty years of teaching high school and more than ten years of writing romance, the genre I love best in the world.

Which is what Damon Suede and I were talking about when he hoodwinked me into writing this book.

Damon Suede is a powerhouse in Romancelandia—and I've had the privilege of talking romance with him for years. Like me, he has the heart of a teacher and a passion for storytelling, whether it's writing romance or debating the evolution of pop culture during a leisurely lunch.

"So when are you going to teach more?" he asked. "Your students enjoy your classes—you love it. Why aren't you teaching more often?"

"I don't know how to market myself as a teacher. You know I love discussing story and helping people work on their technique, but I barely know how to market myself as a writer, and that's how I make a living!"

"Well, first you write a craft book so people know how much you know."

The idea made me feel a little out of my element. After all, I'm a fiction writer. At the point of this book's publication, I will have published nearly one hundred stories that are category length and longer—and I have a thousand more hiding behind my eyes. But writing nonfiction? It had never occurred to me.

"Like, a how-to book? Like on archetypes or character or setting?" These are all classes I've taught before, but I should have known. Damon had a plan.

"Like on category romance! Duh!"

A thousand years ago, Damon and I had started discussing category romance—and it turns out we both had a passion for reading them.

Where other people saw a small pulpy novel—short fiction, a bored housewife's last recourse—we saw something much more detailed. We saw a perfectly crafted nugget of storytelling, a carefully structured truffle of conflict layered on character, layered on plot.

I cannot count the number of discussions we'd had about how perfect a well-written category romance could be, how it could live in a reader's heart a lot longer than on the pulp paper it was written on, and how the craftsmanship and literary awareness of those little word confections were constantly underestimated by the people who dismissed them with a haughty sniff. "Grocery-store romances," they'd say— without realizing that in order to sell in a grocery store, that book, those writers, that imprint, had to be selling like *gangbusters* in a thousand different places, and that this art form had to generate a tremendous, multifaceted appeal before it ever graced the hallowed halls of Safeway.

So Damon must have had all this in mind when he said, "You've read them all your life, you love them, and you've written a bunch that have sold really well. I think that's your new mission in life." He looked at my husband. "Don't you?"

My Mate is easily led. "Yes—I've been telling her that for years."

I sputtered. "My schedule! My deadlines! My—"

"Do it while you wait for your kids to finish dance class. What I'm saying is that we need a user-friendly category romance book—written by someone who understands the mechanics and is willing to lay it down for writers who want to grok it better. Too many people think that category is all about shortness and clichés—"

"Oh, I hate that! It's a very specific thing! It's about choosing a trope and following it through and knowing all of the associations of that trope so that people aren't just reading the shortened romance, they're reading the depth of expectations that readers have for those particular elements of romance. It's like fiction haiku—"

He smiled, catlike. "Fiction haiku. Just write what you know. You'll have a blast."

"You'd better beta read," I grumbled. It was already half-written in my head.

Thanks, Damon—for spending a lunch with me and my Mate, for encouraging me to do wonderful things, for believing I am fully capable of doing them with no questions asked. That kind of faith is a kind of magic.

I'll never take it for granted.

A Word About the Notebook

I OFFER a variety of exercises in this book, some at the end of chapters, some right there in the middle. I will usually say something like, "Grab your trusty notebook and jot that down!"

I am going to make a confession.

I have several notebooks in my house that have one page of scribbled notes in them, often half ripped out and sometimes with telephone numbers printed on top. And yet I've published more than ninety books and novellas, several of them category-style romances.

I don't know what to tell you. Honestly, that's just me.

It is *not* most of the people—most of the truly successful people—I write with.

So when I say, "Get your notebook and..." I could be talking about a real notebook. I could be talking about something with lovely handmade paper and a rough finish, using a fountain pen with artistic blotches. I could be talking about a twenty-five-cent spiral notebook available by the gross at Staples right before school starts and a Sharpie. I could be talking about a Word file on your computer.

The fact is, it doesn't matter what shape or form your prewriting exercises take. Concrete, electronic, or a long plotting session between you and your bestie—or you and your cat.

But for people who need notebooks, the prompt to use the notebook is there.

For people who don't? Well, I pity you all, especially if, like me, you tend to write long series, which means you spend extended exploratory sessions reading your own backlist going, "Dammit! What color were this guy's eyes again?"

I'll imagine people reading this with a notebook in hand and be happy for them. For one thing, those truly successful people I know usually have a thousand story ideas *already written down*. This book gives you some shortcuts to thinking about romance—hopefully, if you do a few exercises involving tropes or modeling or even determining what kind of romance you want to write, you will have story ideas ready and waiting for you when the well is dry.

For another thing, you will have a record of the things you've learned as you start your journey as a romance writer. All *I* have are anecdotes and a backlist. When I pulled *this* book together, so much would have been made simpler if I'd kept a notebook detailing my process as I learned the nuts and bolts of writing.

As you investigate writing category romances, I wish you a thousand story ideas and enough good experience to someday be able to tell students, "Yes, when I started to write category, this is what I learned...."

CRAFTING CATEGORY ROMANCE

THE ART OF FICTION HAIKU

Amy Lane

CHAPTER 1:

FICTION HAIKU—HOW TO STAGE AN OPERA IN A PHONE BOOTH

*I am a popular writer and proud of it…. And I really
believe in the category romances. I was there with two
young kids, and the shorter format saved my sanity. I
remember exactly what it felt like to want to read and
not have time to read 200,000 words.*

Nora Roberts
Publishers Weekly,
February 23, 1998

CONSIDER THE HAIKU

I DON'T know about you, but when I was in school, I was always
frustrated by the teachers who told us that "haiku is the hardest poem
to write."

It was a math game, right? Five syllables, seven syllables, five
syllables—done. Now give me an epic poem—that was some meat.
And several relatives who read my hand-printed twenty-four-page
epic poem can testify that they really wished I had stuck to haikus.

But as I got older—and symbolism and allegory and metaphor
started to seep into my thick head—I realized that the math wasn't in
the syllable count, it was in the word choice. And that the expectations
of a haiku poem were more complicated than numbers.

Every word in a haiku was precisely chosen in order to create
the maximum emotional effect. Each word had to do double and triple

and quadruple duty. It wasn't just a noun, a verb, or an adjective—and there was no room for adverbs at this party. Each word was also a concept, a mood, a metaphor, and the way it played off the other words in the poem made it mean more than just itself.

Think of a hieroglyphic or a tarot card. The picture has meaning, but depending on its position in the overall frame or hand or the pictures that surround it, the meaning changes radically. In one hand, the queen of cups can be encouraging you to open your senses and engage your empathy, and in the other, she can be telling you to protect yourself because too much empathy can hurt. In one hand, the ten of coins can be a celebration of good fortune, but in another, it might be a warning to get off your ass and do something because you can't rest on your laurels forever.

This quality of representing more than one thing depending on the surrounding symbols is called *zeugma* or *polysemy.* The words aren't necessary to memorize (although they do sound cool at parties!), but they do give you a sense of the complexity of the idea. If you take a powerful adjective, with layers of meaning behind it, and couple it with a powerful noun, one that has its own lexicon as well, the meaning of both words changes drastically with the pairing.

And when you change one of those words, the meaning changes again.

Take the word *blind.*

Blind as an adjective means "to be without sight." It's a very simple word to comprehend—and thus a very powerful one. To be deprived of one of our five senses diminishes our power in one area, and that's frightening. To have no sense of sight in a sighted world changes our human experience profoundly.

So profoundly, in fact, that the word *blind* is often used metaphorically—not of being deprived of *physical* sight, but of being deprived of emotional or intellectual sight. Because being blind is such a powerful word physically, it becomes even *more* powerful when used as a metaphor—and it impacts the nouns it is used in conjunction with.

For example, a worm, something without power to start with, is rendered even less powerful in conjunction with blind. A blind worm is lowly (and a sighted worm is creepy: just saying). Now, change that to a king. If someone with tremendous power is deprived of the ability to see his kingdom, his situation is both terrible and broken because it's more about being deprived of *insight* than of actual sight.

So a blind king is tragic—but if we change the noun in the sentence, the word blind means different things when ineracting with a different noun. A blind lover is not interpreted as a lover without sight—it's interpreted as a lover who cannot *understand whom they love*. A blind child may have the ability to see but may be sheltered from all the world has to show. A blind mother… well, we'd need at least one more word to write that story.

In word math, A + B does *not* equal C. A + B = earth, and A + C= love, and A + D = death.

Word math is *much* more exciting than algebra—and much trickier too.

"You know," I muttered to myself during college, "they should have lexicons or thesauruses or something so that every weighted word, every *important* word, also has the many synonyms and meanings that attach to it."

And it turns out, they *do*. In fact, in Japan, haiku thesauruses were incredibly valuable, added to generation after generation as poets came into their own and used the language in new and different ways. Each new meaning of a word would be considered carefully and inscribed with precision. Each new connection between words was recorded—generations knew which poet first said love was a rose, and which one said it was a sunset, and which one said it was a ring of fire. But they did not know what *today's* poet would compare it to next—or what the blind king would be doing with the ring of fire that had never been done before.

Think of haiku as a three-dimensional puzzle. Each word is the tip of the iceberg. All of that inherited meaning is below it. Under the obvious image, the surface of the words, the icebergs intertwine, and the word-and-metaphor dance becomes that much more complex. It's a magic trick, a narrative illusion. It's like a cloak with hidden pockets. We all know the shape of the cloak, and we understand that it's to keep us warm—but in every fold there's a nuance or a hidden understanding that makes the garment more than it seems.

Let's look at our blind king again. We've already established that someone with all the power in the world who's oblivious to some sort of truth is a tragic figure. What happens if we give him something to do?

The blind king grasps the
Rose and pricks himself on thorns.
He tastes his own blood.

It's bad, I know—I never claimed to be a poet. But a rose is a universal symbol of both love and pain. A symbol of power who cannot see what he's reaching for hurts himself—and is impervious to the beauty of what he holds. If he can't see the rose as a vessel of love, he's going to see it as an insult, as an injury. And he's powerful. When the powerful—and oblivious—are injured, the consequences can be grave indeed.

What happens after a king feels injured? Is he given a taste of his own blood?

Well, that's the subject of many, many epic poems—but in something so short, what matters is that the weight of it is felt at the end of the statement. We know the epic poem that comes after the blind king tastes his own blood—we've read it in history books and literature, we've seen it in movies, we've even seen it on the news.

That is the tango of icebergs beneath the surface of a blind king in a rose garden. It's much bigger than a man in a fur robe picking flowers—it becomes the terrible dance of power and emotion that has all but crippled the world for millennia.

Given all of that to consider, fitting that idea in seventeen syllables is really quite an extraordinary feat.

NOW CONSIDER THE CATEGORY ROMANCE

A CATEGORY romance is, quite simply, a romance published under a particular set of requirements—or category.

The number of categories varies by publisher and imprint, but each category is branded differently, marketed differently, and appeals to a different range of readers—older readers might remember Silhouette Desire or Harlequin Presents. Younger readers have most likely seen Harlequin Candlelight Romance or Blaze. That long-ago discussion with my grandfather notwithstanding, not all romances are the same, and a category romance is a way for a reader to get exactly what they want by selecting the branding that appeals to them.

Some of the parameters set around category romances can include:

Length: 40-60,000 words? 60-80? People have different preferences, and some stories take more or fewer words to tell. Setting category romances by length helps readers know what sort of time commitment they're making—and romance readers are a busy group. They want to know they have time to read the story, and they need to know the time frame for the story will give them a complete reading experience. Time is important.

Subgenre: Paranormal? Romantic suspense? Small-town? Historical? And even, sometimes, a subgenre of a subgenre. Paranormal romantic suspense? Cowboys only? Regency? Depending on time period and demand, there have been some very specific categories out there.

Sensuality level: No-holds-barred, all the sex words, blow-back-the-hair-and-steam-up-the-glasses sexy? Slow burn with sweet, suggestive sex? Fade to black? No on-page sex, period, and definitely no sex before marriage? No matter what your preference, oh yes—since the 1980s, there has been a category for that.

Trope: There is a romance category that features sharp city girls and one that features second-chance romance. This entire book is about tropes because tropes are such an integral part of our imaginary lives that they don't just impact the genre we love, they've helped create it. Category romances can revolve around trope just as easily—and as tightly—as they revolve around sensuality level and subgenre.

No matter how you slice, dice, or compartmentalize a romance book, there's a category for that.

For many years, category offered the simplest path to publication—mostly because so many books were needed to satisfy the reading base. A category author could get a bigger print run based on the series requirements alone. Because the quality was expected to be uniform, the editors were absolutely adamant about the series guidelines. Therefore, category worked as a training ground for newer authors who would gradually work their way up to longer "single title" romance. Well, times have changed. Nowadays publishers and audiences seek out category romances on their own merits… because they are uniquely suited to the intense pace and demands of the twenty-first-century publishing market.

Category romances are marketed very clearly—they have uniform branding, uniform size, character-driven cover art, and titles that specifically convey the tropes featured between the covers. One of my favorite examples of a trope-driven title is *The Greek Tycoon's Green-Card Groom*, written by Kate McMurray. One look at the handsome billionaire on the cover and you know that this story is about a marriage of convenience… between two men. And it even rhymes! No reader would pick this story up by accident without knowing what they were in for. One glance at the cover would do it.

But even if the reader *did* pick this story up by accident and didn't know what they were in for, there should still be relatively few surprises. They picked up a category romance—it's going to have two engaging main characters, deploy classic romance tropes, and feature a strong, exciting writing voice that reinvents these tropes while honoring them at the same time, then culminate in that most paramount of requirements: the happy ending.

This is a romance. Every word, every kiss, every yearning glance must convey the one thing the romance reader craves beyond all else.

A thread of hope.

Seems simple? Well, a simple creation can be both perfect to behold and frustratingly difficult to achieve.

The following are some things a category romance is *not*.

1. IT IS NOT A ROMANCE NOVEL THAT JUST HAPPENS TO BE SHORTER.

In fact, length itself—including classifications of more than 85,000 words—makes up part of each book's category. The shorter titles are expected to pack the same amount of punch as the longer titles. Every component—character, conflict, trope—needs to be compressed. It's not short because it's easy, it's short because it's precisely the length the reader enjoys. Write to craft the right story for the right length.

2. IT IS NOT SLOPPILY WRITTEN.

Category romance features evergreen tropes, a small cast, and a tight plot that doesn't allow for subplots, digression, or elaborate world building. They demand precision, conciseness, and invention within a form as standardized as a sonnet and as pragmatic as a shopping list. Category audiences have specific expectations about tone, topic, and tropes. Savvy category authors write to be on target.

3. IT IS NOT WRITTEN FOR THE UNINTERESTING, THE IGNORANT, OR PEOPLE WITH NOTHING MEANINGFUL IN THEIR LIVES.

Category romance readers are very often college-educated, and often have spouses, jobs, children, hobbies, and lives that never slow down. They don't read because they have nothing else to do. They read because, like every other human on earth, they crave stories to stimulate their thinking, their emotions, and their empathy. They don't prefer short fiction because they're lazy; often they read it because they have very little time—or crave that hit of happy whenever they can get it. One of my favorite fan letters ever was from a prosecuting attorney who was reading one of my books on the train on the way home at the end of a long week. He said it was the only time he remembered laughing all day. That is your category romance reader. If you bore that person, you lose him or her, you lose future sales, and you lose your publisher. Write to be interesting.

4. IT IS NOT DUMBED-DOWN LONG ROMANCE.

It is carefully crafted expectation-specific romance. Yes, it is created from familiar tropes, but it's important to understand them because they *are* familiar. If you write a trope wrong, your readers will crucify you, you will lose potential sales, and you will lose your publisher. Write to fulfill hopes.

5. IT IS NOT CLICHÉD PROSE.

Clichéd prose is boring. And remember, your reader doesn't have time to be bored. If you use standard clichés in your prose, you will lose your reader, lose your future sales, and lose your publisher. Write to be fresh.

6. IT IS NOT COMPLETELY PREDICTABLE.

Yes, there are a limited number of tropes, and your reader will be familiar with all of them. But it is up to you to write them in a way a reader hasn't seen before—or in a way that feels fresh, even if it's an homage to a time-honored tradition. Are you writing a virgin? Do they have to be shy? Awkward? Embarrassed? Can't they just be busy, and it takes a really amazing significant other to awaken the need to make some time for sex, love, intimacy? Today's lovers are pretty savvy about sex, so today's romance heroes and heroines should be the same. If you write outdated romance characters, you will bore your reader, lose potential sales, and hogtie your publisher. Write to delight!

TROPES: THE CORE OF CATEGORY ROMANCE

A TROPE is a recurring plot or character device that identifies a genre or subgenre. It's a signal to a reader, telling them what they can expect from their reading experience.

Tropes are easily recognizable. A prince and a waitress is a plot device you've heard of before, and any variation thereof will ping your radar. If you've ever watched a movie and said, "Why does Hollywood always have characters do that?", you are recognizing a trope—and probably a hackneyed one if you're asking that question. But the fact is, you've seen that trope before, and you recognize what the characters have to do before the movie finishes. You can map the kind of journey this story offers and know the kinds of emotions it will make you feel. And that brings us to the inevitable question: How do I provide a fresh reading experience if I'm bound by plot devices and characters that my readers are already familiar with?

Freshness is the reason category operates as a kind of fiction haiku: reader expectations make up the bulk of the writing. The writer is left to provide engaging characters, sparkling dialogue, and smooth execution. Jane Austen, Alexandre Dumas, and Charles Dickens *reveled* in tropes, but those expected elements freed their voices and vision in ways that made them legends. Hidden princes, rescued orphans, and lovers who clash at first sight were hardly new devices even when those authors wrote—but *The Count of Monte Cristo*, *Oliver Twist*, and *Pride and Prejudice* have altered the way we look at literature forever. Everybody knows what to expect with a cheese plate, but there's a difference between freshly baked brie with some garlic and bleu cheese crumbles and a handful of shredded cheddar from a bag.

Each plot trope and character trope isn't *just* a device. It's not *just* a theme or a job or a character description we've seen before. Each trope signals *layers of meaning under the surface* of the character or plot device as it occurs. Each syllable/detail/element packs several punches, because it *must*, to satisfy the reader.

If your character trope is "hero with a tragic past," that's wonderful—everybody loves a good tragic past. It's your job to write the tragic past, the lover's specific reaction to it, the path to redemption that will free them from their torment, and the thing that the hero's significant other brings to the table that helps to complete and release Tragic Protagonist from the pain of repeated mistakes. With a few words in the blurb, the reader knows to prepare for some sniffles and for the great cathartic release at the end. It's like knowing what kind of cereal you're getting because there's a picture of bright sugar marshmallows on the front.

The trope is familiar, yes. *But everything else is you.* That's your blind king, as it were. We know the definition of blind and we know the definition of king, but when you put them together, they create something different. In this case, we know what a hero is supposed to do to fulfill their role, and we know the many forms a tragic past can take. The author's job is to provide specifics in such a way that the reader will be surprised. "Oh, I knew there was something, but that just broke my heart!"

You must ask yourself, is the king's love going to be a rose, a sunset, or a ring of fire? *That is all you.*

Yes, the tropes have been written. I mean, hey, there are *lists*, right? But how they interact and engage is all on you. That's your *job*.

What's also your job is to discover a new hook, a new way to pull readers into what is essentially the world's oldest story: lovers love. It really is the tale as old as time. But who loves, how they love, what stands in the way of their love—that changes, and it gives old tropes new twists every day.

Are you ready? Then let's get started.

NOTEBOOK TIME: VISUALIZE HAPPY

SO IT'S time to think about your favorite romances—and visualize happy. This is an activity that can help you get started on your next project if you don't have a couple in your mind to work with yet. In Appendix C, you will find a summary of each exercise in worksheet form so you don't have to wade through my woo-woo instructions every time you want to use it.

When I taught English, I often had students read a work and—à la the Jane Schaffer method of writing an essay—boil it down to two evocative, contrasting, complementary words. Emotion words. *Power* words. Then, whether the students had to write their essay or not, they had begun the internal process necessary to talk about the work in an intelligent, thoughtful manner.

This following exercise is that idea in reverse.

Now, you might already feel inspired—in fact, that's probably why you want to write a category romance in the first place. This exercise goes back to the thing that inspired you. Your thought process needs to go back to a couple of words—a couple of emotions— and it's important to have more than one. One is an absolute. Two or three emotions are like a noun, a verb, and an adjective—their coexistence in the same space changes the nature of what they are. These complementary emotions can generate friction and thought and imagination inside of you. We're going to start with those words.

Close your eyes—or stare out into space—and think about the book you're planning to write. Don't outline it. Don't plan it yet. Just imagine it. Then get out your trusty notebook and get ready.

How does it make you feel?

We're writing romance—it *should* make you feel *happy*. But what kind of happy? There's a lot of flavors of happy going on out there—it's like Cold Stone Creamery. You don't just have Bubblegum Happy, you have Bubblegum Happy with Chopped-up Gummi Bears and Fruity Pebbles Happy. Is your happy bubblegum flavored? Is it sunset flavored? Day at the beach happy? On the couch by a roaring fire in December happy? Champagne and strawberries and a hotel room you don't have to clean happy?

Remember, happy is a complex flavor. Some people love vanilla ice cream, but only a specific vanilla ice cream. Some people prefer raspberry and dark chocolate gelato. Be specific about the tenor and complexity of your happy—feel free to use contrasting adjectives or nouns.

Two or three adjectives or nouns—or even verbs.

Make your decision and write down your chosen words. These words are the answer to the following question:

What flavor of happy am I writing?

Boom. Those emotion words are your flavor. Now you have to decide what ingredients make up that flavor.

Ask yourself the following questions:

What time and place give me this happy?

If you like your happy with a mysterious edge, you're going to want some mysterious locations. If you like haunted-house stories, stuff goes down at night in a lonely manse. If you're all about camping in the woods, choose your trees and terrain, and if you prefer civilization, pick your favorite hotel. The entire book doesn't need to happen there, but you are adding flavors to your happy ice cream. Make them as specific as you dare.

What people give me this happy?

Cowboys and ice skaters? Horse ranchers and ex-soldiers? Computer programmers and sci-fi geeks? What people give you the flavor of happy you're looking for? Do they have to *match* the setting? Can they contrast? Sometimes I love the hard-bitten PI from the bad neighborhood in a swank hotel, surprised to find he likes champagne. Sometimes it's a shy accountant and a hot, confident athlete on a mountainside—but that's my flavor of happy. What's *yours*?

What adventures give me this happy?

You do not have to be writing *Hawaii Five-O* for your characters to have adventures. They can be campers who get lost, nurses who have a rough day on the job, or horse ranchers caught in a flood. A teacher who loses his job for teaching *Harry Potter*, a business student who babysits his crush's seven-year-old, or a businesswoman who finds herself unexpectedly pregnant—this is your book. It is choose your own adventure. You're not locking things in stone, but you *are* identifying what you want in your Happy Sundae. Get wild, get creative, get granular.

Now look at your answers to the questions.

- *What flavor do you want your happy to be?*
- *Where and when might you find that flavor in the world?*
- *Which characters give you that happy?*
- *Which adventures offer that happy?*

Keep these answers—and do this exercise as often as you like. Depending on your mood, the movie you just watched, the book you just read, the answers will change, and every set of answers is an idea to start with.

Also, I would bet, when we get to the lists of tropes, you will see your flavors of happy listed there. You may even see some of the same combinations.

But I would wager, when all is said and done, that your happy— no matter which flavor—will not taste the same as anybody else's.

As we continue to talk about the ingredients of a category romance writer's Happy Sundae, remember, every writer—whether they write genre fiction or literary fiction—is going to use tropes in his or her work. The artistry of category romance lies in making those tropes unique and different. Just like you could send an entire romance writers conference into Cold Stone Creamery and not have the same ice cream repeated twice, you could have ten romance writers choose the same theme, setting, character tropes, and plot tropes, and not one of them would write the same book.

That's our job, right? To make love just as sweet, just as satisfying, and just as surprising, *every single time*.

For those of you who keep a writing notebook, you may want to put this list of questions—or any questions that inspire you—on the top of each page or section. It's a way to boil your project down to the emotions you want it to invoke. Finding the feeling or rush you want to bring your reader is an amazing way to train your imagination to play with your project again and again.

Personally? When I'm in the car, or walking the dogs, or doing the dishes, if I think about those key emotion words, I find myself immersed immediately in my project. Feel free to use this—or any other visualization method you can find—to put yourself in the mindset to chase your own happy.

CHAPTER 2:

CHARACTER—THE PEOPLE ON ROMANCE LANE

A lot of the times in real life, there's nothing more than our own backstories that keep us from falling in love. So I incorporate that into my books. Family. Loss. Unrest. Drama.

Jill Shalvis
All About Romance blog
June 26, 2016

I'M GOING to describe someone for you.

Meet Dave.

Dave is an assistant soccer coach.

Dave is six feet two inches tall, with skin of a gentle brown, and eyes as dark and limpid as infinity pools at midnight. His smile is wide and charming, and he has a square jaw, a straight nose, and—are you ready for it?—dimples.

Dave is, in short, dreamy.

He is the fun coach. Dave is the cheerleader on the sidelines getting the girls pumped up and their teamwork functioning.

Does Dave interest you yet? Can you write Dave as a hardworking single father? The coach everybody loves? An interesting person in your neighborhood?

Now, I'm going to add one more ingredient to Dave.

Dave works as a SWAT team commander of the local police force. His day job involves eighty pounds of gear and making the neighborhood safer for everybody involved.

And *that* is the cherry on the Dave sundae.

Dave could be a real person—I'm sure he rang a few bells for a lot of you. But everything about Dave is also a character trope: Single Father, Coach, Adorable Guy-Next-Door, Law Enforcement Officer, Dimples.

Now, if *you* are writing Dave, you might want to fiddle around with him—and take that however you want. Maybe he's *not* an Adorable Guy-Next-Door—maybe he's an angsty neurotic mess driven by A Tragic Secret Backstory. Maybe he's not a Single Father. Maybe he's a Doting Uncle. Maybe he's a Dedicated After-School Tutor. Maybe he's the Mysterious Neighbor. My Dave has a charming smile and laughs at a heroine's jokes. Maybe *your* Dave has a guarded, measured gaze and no sense of humor.

The point here is, *your Dave is your Dave.*

Interesting characters—people a reader could not only imagine meeting but would love to meet—are a compelling part of a romance writer's unique voice and vision for what makes a love story an absolute must-read.

And you can write a fully fleshed-out character—a Dave whom you feel like you know personally—and still utilize character tropes. They're character tropes because they happen so often they're familiar—utilizing the familiar is not a crime. Tropes are shorthand—a person can look at the back of the romance cover and see *Law Enforcement, Single Father, Coach, Dimples*—and know whether or not this could be their favorite flavor of happy.

To look at a real person and create a romance character is not much of a stretch. There needs to be a nugget of reality in all of our fantasies or readers won't be able to suspend disbelief long enough to fall in love. But looking at a character and finding their tropes is a different mental exercise.

Using Dave as an example, unless I was looking at him with my romance brain on, I'd see a nice guy in my neighborhood. But looking at him with some awareness of the engines that drive a romance book as a whole, I see the things about him with broader appeal.

Law Enforcement is a big trope in romance books—generally, we like to be protected, and the Law Enforcement trope gives us the secure knowledge that this character wants to protect people. But that protective instinct comes with drawbacks—it can often be too controlling, and that's a conflict that many readers enjoy reading about.

Not every reader loves the Single Father trope, but the ones who do are *fierce* about it. Watching a big strong man or woman (hey, a *protector*) be tender—or learn to be tender—and cute and fun and steady and all of things that are needed from a good parent is a study in contrasts. Add in Law Enforcement with the possibility of *too* much protection, and people want to know how that person is going to find love!

And someone who's a mentor in the community can be *very* attractive. This person gives his time not just to his child, but to make the world a better place.

One of the biggest criticisms of category romance is that the characters aren't real. That's not true. The characters are as real as we can make them. But as we look at the people we make—or the people we're basing our fictional characters on—we're not just transcribing a guy we know onto the paper. We're transforming him to something that has romantic expectations and universal appeal. This doesn't mean his character is flat because he represents some solidly entertaining romance tropes. He's as detailed as he was before, but now he's pulling the weight of romance expectations behind him, and those expectations are doing some of the talking and entertaining for him. By exploring tropes and expectations, category romance finds the gold in our own backyard. Its charged compression exposes the romantic, dramatic, and magical possibilities in the people we see (or *don't* see) every day.

Dave's a busy guy—he's got a job, a kid, he coaches soccer. He can't be expected to do all of the heavy lifting in the category romance. The reader has to bring their own expectations to the table to see how he meets, exceeds, or defies them. In each character, the writer finds emotional treasure to share with an audience who is greedy for a much-needed escape.

DOUBLE DUTY

CHARACTER TROPES do more than just signal to a reader what the characters are going to be like—they also drive plot.

When Sue Brown-Moore, the former editor of Dreamspinner Press's Dreamspun Desires and Dreamspun Beyond imprints, was asked what she most wished new category writers knew, she had this to say:

> *Let tropes and themes drive the conflict. Don't make a character an FBI agent unless he gets to show off his skills. Because the word count is small, it's okay to go with what comes naturally (like above). Embrace the tropes and find ways within them to differentiate the story. Don't be afraid to be predictable. It's category romance. They're going to meet, feel a spark, get together, be pulled apart, then come back together. Just make the characters memorable and lovable. People read it for the characters, not their struggles.*

She's talking about character tropes and the power of compression—this is the essence of fiction haiku. Dave the SWAT commander with dimples is a great guy as a coach, but what does his job do for the plot? If you're writing forty to sixty thousand words, you don't want to waste any of them on his job unless there's a conflict built into it. What if Dave's love interest is a public defense attorney? That could definitely cause some conflict—and that's another character trope. What if his assistant coach—or a rival coach—was wrongly convicted and is looking for redemption and a second chance?

So. Much. Conflict.

Conflict drives your reader to turn pages, it drives the plot, it gives us an obvious signpost for when the romance can proceed to its preordained destination into the sunset. Conflict is *hugely* important. And if you are writing in shorthand, you can establish major conflict just by choosing your character tropes with care.

THE POWER OF FOILS

WE'VE ESTABLISHED that a character is just the tip of the trope iceberg.

Great—but an iceberg sailing majestically alone in a dark sea is a pretty picture without a lot to do.

Once we've established the character's tropes, we need to figure out who the character is best suited to be with—and here's the fun part: it can't be someone *exactly the same*. There is nothing less exciting than characters who have nothing to clash over, which means they can't be too much alike, and they can't be so different that nobody cares what they do together either.

They have to have just enough common ground to want to figure out how to build a house there. We need to see the best qualities of one character reflected in the other, and the big loneliness-shaped hole in each person that the other character fills.

We are, in short, looking for a *foil*.

In fiction, a foil is another character who shows us what is either abundant or deficient in the main character. Harry Potter has Draco Malfoy, Elizabeth Bennet has Charlotte Lucas, her sister Jane, and Caroline Bingley, and Hamlet has Laertes, Fortinbras, and Horatio. But in the context of romance fiction, a character foil takes on an entirely different—and much more important—function.

A romantic foil is not just the love interest, it is the character who shows us most acutely what the other character is missing. And then fills that space using as few words as possible.

Say our Single Father, Law Enforcement, Community Servant character is too controlling and overwhelmed with responsibility at the same time.

His romantic foil would be someone with maybe not enough control, who avoids responsibility—but is less overwhelmed. Together these two characters create a unit. They fit into each other's missing pieces; they complete the puzzle of the other. They show us the best qualities of the other and alleviate the worst qualities in themselves.

By choosing the right character and plot trope, an author uses shorthand to explain how these two lovers complete each other. Yes, there is still dialogue and character development, but the extensive setup normally needed to explain how two such different people can really create a life together is diced fine by the reader's expectations that they *will* find their way together, because the audience can assess the situation from the trope.

The reader can easily see that these two lovers are perfect for each other. They watch every engagement with the ready knowledge of what conflicts lie ahead, and are delighted when the writer surprises them. Yet, at the same time, they are completely satisfied with the ending that was laid out for them all along.

And there is something satisfying about finding the common ground between two people who complement but don't copy each other. Matching the homebody with the world traveler, the ex-grifter with the content farmer, the shy introvert with the foot-in-mouth spaz—these are the matches nobody saw coming but nobody can imagine any differently.

There is a place for a foil in every trope—because a perfect foil can come from many facets of each character's personality. Are you writing about the homebody? Yes, his foil could be a world traveler. Or, his foil could be a friend who *wants* to travel the world with the homebody by his side. His foil could be somebody new to town with a lot of stories to tell, or someone just around the corner who feels alone in the world of the familiar. There are a lot of ways we can show the homebody the way to adventure—and each way leads to a different foil.

Let's go back to our blind king again. The blind king doesn't necessarily need a flash of *sight*—he just needs *insight*. Insight can come through his four other senses. He can "hear the music," "taste victory," "smell freedom," or "feel a path before him." Establishing a foil or opposite character trope to complete a romantic hero doesn't have to be an obvious or predictable choice.

Readers love surprises—as long as they make sense. A foil always makes sense, but it's not always the obvious choice.

ARCHETYPES AS FOILS

I TEACH a class about western heroic archetypes as romance heroes, and I use the progression of the archetypes throughout literary history to identify their audience-anticipated goals—and how those goals impact their love lives.

The core of this class (which deserves its own book) is the *heroic agenda*—a hero's driving set of internal goals. One sure way to define a possible foil for a character is to identify the hero's goals and find goals that appear to be diametrically opposed.

And then—with the use of character interaction—to show us that the goals *can be* compatible, but only with compromise.

Examples?

Superman:

> Lois Lane wants to uncover the truth.
>
> Clark Kent wants to conceal his identity.
>
> *Both* of them want to reveal the bad guy and stop him.

Black Panther:

> T'Challa wants to keep Wakanda's wealth a secret.
>
> Nakia is willing to expose the secret for the good of her people.
>
> *Both* of them want to further their people and make the entire world a better place.

Pride and Prejudice:

> Elizabeth Bennet wants to save her family from embarrassment so her sisters can marry as they please, so she needs to keep her crush on Mr. Wickham to herself.
>
> Mr. Darcy wants to save his sister from embarrassment because she is young and easily hurt, so he is reluctant to share Mr. Wickham's perfidy.
>
> Both of them want to keep Mr. Wickham from venturing on to harm any other young woman's reputation and chances for the future.

Crazy Rich Asians:

> Rachel Chu wants to find a happy-ever-after with both her boyfriend *and* his family.
>
> Eleanor Young wants her son, Nick, to choose somebody richer and more appropriate for his social class.
>
> *Both* of them want what's best for Nick.

Now those familiar with the *Superman* and *Black Panther* canons or *Pride and Prejudice* or *Crazy Rich Asians* will recognize that these goals are vastly simplified. Complex characters can have pages upon pages of agenda—which will, of course, give them and their foils pages upon pages of things to talk about. But in the world of trope romance—particularly the compressed short forms of romance—our characters need agendas that deal with universal themes. The author has limited space to convince us that these two people can fall in love. The reader needs to be given enough information to imagine that dialogue, those disagreements, the nature of that compromise. The author has given us the trope and the memorable characters to live it—every conversation they have is going to stem organically from their personalities and those specific agenda items.

Just like in real life, where a few hours in the airport is enough to establish a friendship for the ages, but five years in the same office cannot make two people any more compatible.

Unless, of course, that's your story, in which case there's a trope for that too.

NOTEBOOK TIME:
PEEL BACK THE FOIL

AND BACK to our notebooks. Make a heading called *Character Foils* and then make two columns under that for two lists.

List 1: *What do my characters have in common?*

List 2: *How are my characters different?*

It doesn't matter how you phrase your lists or how you set them up—they're your lists. But when you're done, go back and look at them and remember…

What your characters have in common brings them together.

Their differences drive them apart.

EXAMPLE: *PRIDE AND PREJUDICE*

WHAT DO THE CHARACTERS HAVE IN COMMON?	HOW ARE THE CHARACTERS DIFFERENT?
Age	One is impulsive, one is steady
Country and Social Circle	One is vivacious, one is taciturn
Integrity	One is poorer, one is very wealthy
Belief in family	One was raised with knowledge of extreme responsibility, one was told her responsibility was to marry
Pride in their own conduct	One trusts human nature, one distrusts it in the extreme
Prejudice against the others	
Quickness to anger	
Eventual willingness to forgive	

Now if you're feeling *really* excited about this exercise, look at your two lists and create an agenda statement like the ones above. Remember to look at the things the characters will perceive as differences, the things they think make them absolutely incompatible.

Main character 1's agenda is...

Main character 2's agenda is...

Now think about how their differences can be resolved in one sentence. Just one. How do you make their contrasting desires into a single compatible idea? You may have to go back and rewrite their agendas—their similarities and differences—but you need to come to that one sentence. That's their happy-ever-after right there. It's important.

CHARACTER	AGENDA
ELIZABETH BENNET	Wants to save her family from embarrassment so her sisters can marry as they please, so she needs to keep her crush on Mr. Wickham a secret.
FITZWILLIAM DARCY	Wants to save his sister from embarrassment because she is young and easily hurt, so he is reluctant to share Mr. Wickham's perfidy.
BOTH OF THEM	Want to keep Mr. Wickham from venturing on to harm any other young woman's reputation and chances for the future.

NOTEBOOK TIME:
THE GRAMMAR OF CHARACTERS
SPEAKING

AND NOW that you've decided what drives these people—who are they?

I know it may seem backward, to establish a character's agenda first and who they are second, but the agenda is what drives the character. It's what makes them who they are. Once you've established the agenda, almost everything you need to know—besides hair color, eye color, height, and weight—can be derived from *what drives this character*.

Once you've decided what drives them, summarizing them in a single, unforgettable sentence is the next step.

Did I just hear gasps? Yes. One sentence.

That doesn't mean your character won't have complexities and nuances that will fill a book, but this character is making a big impact in a limited number of words. You have an entire book to explain the character's quirks and foibles, but you have a two-hundred-word blurb or a paragraph-long synopsis to capture an audience's attention.

And once you have their attention, this character must continue to deliver to that expectation for the *entire book*.

There are a couple of ways to parse that character sentence, but since they're basically announcing a character's driving goal, they are almost always wedded together by a verb like *wants, needs, tries, must, can't,* or *demands*. In short, a verb that announces motivation.

Other than that, the sentence is a carefully chosen array of the words you feel showcase your character's most salient features.

A good summary sentence has a couple of descriptors, a powerful noun, and a thing this character *wants, needs, is trying desperately, must, can't,* or *demands* to do.

ADJECTIVE + ADJECTIVE + NOUN PHRASE + WANTS + VERB PHRASE

Pretty, bookish, devoted daughter Belle wants to experience the world beyond her provincial town.

THE ADJECTIVE + NOUN PHRASE + ADVERB PHRASE + WANTS + VERB PHRASE

The angry enchanted beast who lives in the nearby castle wants to be left alone.

NAME + APPOSITIVE + WANTS + VERB PHRASE

Belle Diva—studious daughter of an absentminded inventor—wants nothing more than for her father to succeed in applying for his patent.

NAME + IS + NOUN PHRASE + WHO WANTS + VERB PHRASE

Eric Bheest is an environmentalist who's desperate keep his land from being stripped of its native flora and fauna.

Feel free to play about with form, with grammar, with specific word choices, and even with synonyms for *want*, but remember that in some way, shape or form, the character sentence will *always* be DESCRIPTOR + CHARACTER + THING THEY ARE DESPERATELY TRYING TO DO.

CHARACTER HAIKU

A GRAMMAR formula to outline a character is a handy tool, but remember: word choice is *everything*. Reader expectations are one of a category romance writer's most powerful tools, and when you are describing a character, you have a chance to invoke the full weight of that expectation with every word.

And the way to do this is to utilize the tropes that readers will be looking for when they pick up your book.

But wait, you say. What about my own voice? Isn't that important?

Well, *yes*. Editors are looking for books that sound unique and original—even when they're telling the world's oldest story. A reader is looking for an expected trope, they are not looking to be bored. So your job is to utilize reader expectations to surprise them.

Each trope comes with its own expectation of conflict, with the weight of a hundred movies and a thousand romances that have utilized this character type before. Just like when you're choosing words for a short-form poem or haiku, choosing the *right* trope will engage your reader.

And then twisting it with your own characters, your own dialogue, your own unique interpretation of what romance is, and your special storytelling style will hook them for life.

The following is an (incomplete!) discussion of different character tropes and their expectations for conflict. As you write your one-sentence character descriptions and your character agendas, take a look at this list and decide which tropes you are engaging and what language you can use to trigger reader awareness. Remember, these classic tropes are popular because they engage the heart or the imagination in some way that hasn't faded, even after more than a hundred years of romance literature. Telling people that what you've chosen is the kind of character story they've always loved is a great way to show them how much they'll love the story *you* tell.

CHARACTER TROPES AND THEIR CONFLICTS

BEAUTY AND THE BEAST

One of the characters is sweetness and light and the other is dark and angsty.

Expectation of conflict: Well, it's kind of obvious, but the real challenge is in making the dark and angsty/angry character redeemable. If he's a first-rate prick, we want our Beauty to ditch the Beast and go find a Boy Next Door. Because, really, who needs the aggravation?

BOY OR GIRL NEXT DOOR

This trope is about the character who is pure, wholesome, usually sweet or snarky, and familiar.

Expectation of conflict: This trope's challenge is to get the other main character to see this person, often someone previously known to them, as a sexual being and not just someone sweet, pure, snarky, wholesome, and familiar.

CAST-IRON BOSS

This one is rough. We usually want likeable main characters, but these characters start off prickly, irritating, and mean. There is often a reason for this—Tragic Past, Orphan, Betrayal—as well as plenty of plot tropes that can make a perfectly nice romantic hero or heroine into a total pain in the ass. It's up to the writer to make the character's transition from complete asshole to sympathetic main character believable.

Expectation of conflict: You have a character who is pretty much despised by everybody else in the story—including the other main character. Because of the nature of this person's decisions, they are likely to generate friction with *everybody in the book.*

CINDERELLA

One of the characters has either a low station in life or low self-esteem and needs to debut as beautiful and confident and worthy of love.

Expectation of conflict: Either the "prince" in this story needs to be oblivious—perhaps Cinderella is a Girl/Boy Next Door? Perhaps the "prince" has social or family obligations of marrying someone of his or her station?—or perhaps there's some obstacle in Cinderella's own psyche that makes that debut a true transformation.

ENEMIES TO LOVERS

This one belongs in the plot trope category too, but keep in mind that if you pick natural enemies—an animal rights activist with a cattle rancher, for example—you have tapped into people with a lot to talk about who might have the same agenda. In this case, the ethical treatment of animals.

Expectation of conflict: You have established an immediate conflict expectation just by choosing the appropriate job.

FISH OUT OF WATER

This is a character trope that depends on a plot trope. The character needs to be absolutely unsuited for the circumstance—and this is especially effective if *both* characters take a tour in each other's uncharted territory.

Expectation of conflict: Pretty much everything. This is where your characterization and plotting blend seamlessly together, because how a character reacts in unfamiliar waters both drives action and creates more conflict. A strong, interesting Fish Out of Water makes a lot of freakin' waves.

FRIENDS TO LOVERS

This trope might appear in the plot trope category too, but it's here because if you have picked your personality tropes and it appears they'll get along without conflict, you don't really have a book.

Expectation of conflict: The transition from friends to lovers *is* conflict. The pre-established pattern of behavior rubs up against the new normal in every scene.

JADED HEART

This one is the classic character from commedia dell'arte who is older, wiser, and a little bit jaded. The Columbine thinks they are not good enough for the younger virgin or Boy/Girl Next Door.

Expectation of conflict: Your virgin or Boy/Girl Next Door thinks the Columbine is really swell and plans to become absolutely indispensable to this poor old soul, while your Columbine is saying, "You are *awfully* cute, but I am too old and worn and past my prime and… oh wow. Did you bake me cookies?" Mm… I love this trope, I'm not gonna lie. It's one of my favorites.

MARTYR

This trope features somebody so focused on the greater good that they have difficulty acknowledging their own emotional needs.

Expectation of conflict: The martyr sometimes has a Tragic Past or sometimes is just a really good person—but the conflict comes when the other main character asks for relationship time. An example of a martyr could be a doctor, a policeman or firefighter, or even a businessperson who is trying to keep the business afloat for people other than themself.

MISTAKEN SELF-IDENTITY

Is your policeman prone to getting hurt? Is your college academic much more rough-and-tumble than your standard English professor? Is your knitter really an amateur sleuth? If your main character's self-perception is vastly different from his or her actual skill set, their self-identity needs some reevaluation.

Expectation of conflict: When a person reevaluates their entire life, this is an amazing chance to open new doors and start new adventures. But changing an entire life means *everybody* in that person's life needs to change their way of thinking. This is an amazing trope—it usually means that one of the main characters sees something so amazing in the other that his or her own self-perception changes, and together, the two characters become an entirely different entity. But this never comes without cost, and that's an unspoken conflict that will permeate the entire book.

OPPOSITES ATTRACT

Cousin to the Fish Out of Water trope, in this case the two most unlikely people in the world are paired off and discover they have something in common.

Expectation of conflict: Again, just about everything from clothes to philosophies to words that one person uses that the other dislikes. The important thing is that they have enough in common to make the fighting worth it.

ORPHAN

One character is either a literal orphan and is used to making their own place in the world, or they could be a figurative orphan, in that they have been deprived of love.

Expectation of conflict: Someone deprived of love often thinks they are *unworthy* of love, and all sorts of painful behaviors can result.

PROTECTOR

This one fits a lot of the Law Enforcement or Occupation tropes (see the Appendices), in which one character is assigned to protect the other, either from an outside threat to their person, their reputation, or even their family.

Expectation of conflict: Nobody likes to be babysat, and this often puts two strong personalities—with conflicting agendas—in close proximity.

SEXUAL BUTTERFLY

Also a plot trope, a Sexual Butterfly is a character who makes a transformation from being someone who seems plain and unsexual—not unattractive, but simply not a sexual being—into a sensual powerhouse. A librarian who sings torch songs. A stern teacher who exercises by pole dancing. A disapproving boss singing karaoke with well-stuffed tighty-whities. The Sexual Butterfly is someone who spends part of the book transforming from a wallflower into a 24/7 wood-erecting panty-wetter.

Expectation of conflict: This trope presents internal conflict because our Butterfly is discovering new, uncharted depths within themselves, and external conflict because our Butterfly's beloved is going to be *very* surprised. Both parties have to reconcile their previous expectations of the Butterfly with this charming—and sexy—new reality.

STUCK IN A RUT

This one often starts with a job or a setting. Is your character too much of a homebody? A mechanic who wants to own his own business? A dreamer who never acts on his or her dreams? Someone so terribly lonely they don't even know where to start building a family of their own? This trope usually involves stasis, and then an exciting event to get the character moving.

Expectation of conflict: Change is hard. Changing in response to another person entering your life like a rogue billiard ball, smacking you out of your own apathy and into a whole new trajectory, is often accompanied by grumpy banter, hurt feelings, and extremely painful introspection. And, of course, the comfort of the rogue billiard ball, who really had no bad intentions whatsoever.

TERRIBLE SECRET

Much like the Terrible Sin or Tragic Past that follow, this one deals with something in the character's backstory that is impacting their present chances for happiness. The difference with this one is that the Terrible Secret often affects both main characters. The Secret Baby plot trope fits into the Terrible Secret, and so does the I Lied To Protect You trope. The character aspect of the Terrible Secret lies in how each character deals with the perceived betrayal, and the things a person must do to keep a secret bigger than their own heart.

Expectation of conflict: Usually there's a whole lot of baggage in this secret—unpacking those suitcases is going to take us deep into both main characters, and we're going to have a whole lot of grievances to air before they can be civil to each other again.

TERRIBLE SIN

This is a version of the Tragic Past in which the main character is trying to achieve redemption for a perceived wrong committed before the second main character was on the stage.

Expectation of conflict: With the Terrible Sin trope, the person who didn't commit the sin must offer some sort of absolution. If they both committed a Terrible Sin, it's going to be a really long book.

TRAGIC PAST

Obviously the main character has something painful in their past that interferes with the ability to form relationships now.

Expectation of conflict: This trope implies hurt/comfort, redemption, lack of communication, overcoming fears, letting go of resentments, and long, heartfelt talks that build intimacy.

TROUBLE MAGNET

Another plot-trope favorite, this one involves a main character who can't stay out of trouble. This is the friend who goes to the dry cleaner's, stops to feed a homeless child, witnesses a robbery, and ends up running for her life and becoming a foster parent before she comes back. The Trouble Magnet is an active, interesting person who just sort of seems to attract trouble.

Expectation of conflict: First of all, as a friend, this person is annoying as hell. Every trip to the dry cleaner's is fraught with drama, and God forbid they do something *really* exciting, like get stuck on a layover and have to hide in the hotel basement from tornadoes. And as a *significant other*, this person can set the life of a Protector, or an orderly neatnik, or any sane person who is trying to establish a life or a routine, completely on its ear.

But things will never be boring.

UGLY DUCKLING

This is a double-duty trope—it can also be a plot trope. The ugly duckling is just like the Hans Christian Andersen fairy tale. They are ugly and picked upon by ducks, and then become a swan and can essentially either shit on, ignore, or (this is the best option) *forgive* the bullies of their youth.

Expectation of conflict: An ugly duckling's conflict comes from three places—inside themself acknowledging the new inner beauty; with the hero, who is either suddenly seeing our precious duckling in an entirely new way *or* has always seen Ducky as awesome and has been waiting for Ducky to see it too; and with the bullies who have kept Ducky sad and bedraggled and self-hating before the transformation.

VIRGIN AND THE RAKE/PLAYBOY/PLAYER/ BAD BOY

One of them has done it, but one of them hasn't. Sounds simple enough, but….

Expectation of conflict: Your virgin needs to be empowered. Forty years ago, an older, debauched rake seducing a wide-eyed virgin was a perfectly acceptable trope, particularly if the virgin was super stubborn about holding on to her V-card. That's still a fun trope— but modern readers expect more complexity than just a hymen or a hang-up. It needs to be about emotional intimacy versus emotional superficiality, or emotional availability versus emotional isolation. And yes, sometimes it's the virgin who's got the good emotional subset going and the rake who's isolated or superficial. This is a *great trope*—but it can't be about simple seduction anymore.

POPULAR PERSONALITY trope conflicts abound in category romance. Please feel free to add to this list as you read and write more. The point is that for every trope—for every dramatic function or personality expectation—you'll learn to spot a romantic conflict begging to be exploited. If you can craft a character who carries expectations and a personality conflict that plays into that, you have essentially allowed a very few words, a very brief descriptor, to do a massive amount of emotional work for you.

In short, the trick with looking at lists like these is learning to mine them for potential conflicts.

To that end, it's important to look at where conflict comes from—particularly between people who are, in the end, very well suited for each other. This also helps if none of the tropes on that list appeals to you and you resolve to go find your own. Where do you go from here to find the heart of the friction that keeps your reader engaged?

To the heart of conflict—and exactly where it comes from.

SOURCES OF CONFLICT

EXTERNAL CONFLICT is so much easier to write. Oh my God, the levee broke, everybody head for the hills! BOOM! That's a conflict—and a very clear resolution to it. The friction between two people is often more difficult to pinpoint—and it's the secret ingredient that keeps us eating category romances like potato chips. Why can't people just get along? What is it about human beings that makes them clash, and what miracle intervenes to help them find harmony?

To look beyond the trope—or to figure out where your characters and their conflicts are coming from—it's important to examine the things that can get between us when we're destined to be together.

AGENDAS

An agenda is more than a to-do list. It's a set of priorities that a character feels they must accomplish. In my class about heroic archetypes, each hero has a very specific agenda. Sometimes it's to save the village, and sometimes it's to save the hero's crush. Imagine what happens when the hero's crush wants to save the village! Conflicting agendas—big picture versus small picture, the greater good versus the single happy child, the environment versus a tiny struggling business—can be one of the biggest conflicts in any relationship, and they are often built right into the characters' jobs. If you are pairing a Doctors Without Borders worker with a SEAL team member sent to save her, you have just created a *Clash of the Titans*.

BACKGROUND/EDUCATION

Where we come from and how we were educated can shape us in a lot of ways. Even if we reject the conditioning of our youth—maybe *especially* if we reject the conditioning of our youth—our preconceived notions of what someone from the exact same background is supposed to be can cause us to make the worst of assumptions. I would say "Remember the country mouse and the city mouse!" except that Aleksandr Voinov and I wrote books with *that exact trope*—titled *Country Mouse* and *City Mouse*. Contrasting rich and poor or self-educated and Ivy League is the tip of the iceberg. Try contrasting a doctor and a nurse—because those are two very different educations and two very different agendas. Pair up a college-educated architect with a boots-on-the-ground city planner and see what steams up. The minute a reader sees the presented differences, they're going to expect the heat level to reach epic proportions—and there is nothing wrong with that as long as you deliver.

COMMUNICATION

Most of the time it's not possible to resolve character conflicts with one long, heartfelt talk, but that's especially true if the people involved are only good at communicating in grunts and snappy comebacks. Bad Communication—the revealing of what is in one human being's heart to another—is the basis of more broken crockery than who needs to leave the toilet seat down. Having two emotionally closed-off characters find the words to actually let the other person in can be the entire conflict of a category romance *if it's done right*. But even if that's not the central conflict, it's still a source of friction. How the other sources of conflict play out depends on Bad Communication for both surprises and roadblocks in the course of the story.

Remember that by employing well-known character types already in conflict, you are engaging a reader by engaging their life experiences and expectations. And whether you play your characters right into their heads or turn them upside down by giving things a twist, you have to have them immediately, with the familiar. Only then can you dazzle them with the people in your head that nobody else has.

HIERARCHIES

Any job or any field has a pecking order. Any clash of personalities that upsets the usual applecart is going to create an instant, recognizable conflict. Making one character new to the team and the other character set in his or her ways creates instant friction. Military protocol and the rogue operative are always highly entertaining in romance fiction. Find a way for the hierarchy in the job to work for you—it certainly gets in the way enough in real life.

Pay attention to the heroic agendas your heroes' jobs carry with them—they can drive your plot like a freight train.

PHILOSOPHIES

Philosophical differences have broken up more marriages than "Whose turn is it to clean the cat box?" If one of your characters believes animals are people too, and the other believes cows exist for milk and steak, that could be a double homicide waiting to happen or a match made in heaven. Because we're writing romance, it needs to be a match made in heaven. But remember, certain jobs have certain philosophes that come with them. A private investigator with a heart of gold and a win-at-all-costs defense attorney will eventually have a lot of words to shout at each other if they don't find a way for their trains to share the same platform.

PRECONCEIVED EXPECTATIONS

There doesn't need to be a different background for there to be conflicting expectations. If two characters from the same background expect each other to be the worst of their past, that is a weighted set of expectations. The same comes with the biases implanted in us from our youth. Expecting the worst or best of someone when all they have to offer is their human selves can teach a character oceans of life lessons in a couple of memorable scenes.

TIMING/PLANS

One person is just getting out of college—while the other is ready to retire. One person is ready to start a family while the other one has already raised children and is ready to fly. Two people establish an amazing emotional connection just when one of them is flying to wed a fiancé they truly care about. Being in different places in their lives is an obstacle that can really get in the way of a romance—or make two people especially sure they can compromise in order to get the thing they want most in the world, true love.

NOTEBOOK TIME: TROPETASTIC CHARACTER MATH

IT'S TIME for another exercise!

Or, well, time to outline a book, depending on how thorough you want to get.

Take a look at your character foils if you like, or your one-sentence character summary. Remember how I said you could practically write the entire book if you did that part right? It's time to give that a try.

Choose two characters (or go back and make them up if you skipped that part) and look over the character tropes. The rest flows from there.

This first exercise is pretty simple:

1. Choose a Developed Character trope—one of your favorites. Boy Next Door? Sexual Butterfly? If you wrote your characters—and their motivations—specifically enough, you might find that they will lend themselves to something on that list.

2. Take a look at that character. Think about who they are and what they are missing. This isn't their agenda—it's something that can be seen from the outside easier than inside. Decide what this character needs in their life that will make the pain and befuddlement of finding a mate worth it. Jot that down.

3. Go back and look at the Developed Character tropes above. Pretty much every one of them suggests the "other." The Jaded Heart trope suggests a young and chipper Boy or Girl

Next Door for the jaded rake or woman who's seen too much heartbreak. Cinderella needs a patient and dedicated prince. Your Cast-Iron Boss needs someone who can hold their own, but with the compassion to see into the heart of the monster and uncover the hurt human underneath. Find the "other" that completes the first.

4. Choose likely professions, hobbies, or occupations for the characters. I've provided a handy appendix at the end (Appendix A)! Remember that some characters are Mistaken Identity and might need to discover that about themselves.

5. Now list the sources of conflict between those people. This will come completely from your own experience. You're a person, you know people—what drives other people crazy?

Easy? Yes. But you've essentially outlined the beginnings of a story—go you!

This next exercise starts with the above exercise and then builds on it.

Begin with steps 1-5 above.

6. Figure out what the "other" needs that the first character can give them.

7. Develop your characters a little. Give them personality, dialogue, appearance—the list of things that make this person *this person*.

8. Look at the two characters you've generated and highlight the similarities and differences between them. There must be similarities, or these two people have no business being in the same room together. But there should be plenty of differences too.

9. Ask yourself, "What *specific* conflict will these two people generate just by being in the same

room together?" Take a look at the sources
of conflict, if you need to. If you've got two
Protectors in the same room, one from the
sheriff's office and one from the FBI, you have
run into a Hierarchy problem and a Philosophy
problem, and possibly an Agenda problem.
And yet they are both in Law Enforcement—
so they obviously have something in common.
Do what you must do to figure out where the
friction is.

Remember—we're thinking like a poet!

Now is the time to clarify your language and your tropes.

Look back at your characterizations and your trope. Is there
anything you can cut or combine? Do you need to tell us that someone
is protective if you've just told us they work for Law Enforcement? Do
you need to tell us someone is socially conscious when they volunteer
at a soup kitchen? Cut anything extraneous in your characterizations
and remember your simple, powerful vocabulary. Instead of *blind
king*, you're using *Law Enforcement soccer coach* here—your reader
can see the conflicts coming a mile away.

Once your descriptions are simplified and clarified and you
know exactly who you're dealing with, let your characters play with
each other.

*What situation could I put these two people in that would turn
their friction into flame?*

That is where plot comes in, and plot needs conflict. And *that*
leads us to our next chapter.

Chapter 3:

Conflict—Not Just a Glitch in Your Schedule

It's all about the conflict. Conflict is not a situation that can be resolved with a conversation, but, as the amazing Mary Buckham states, it is a clash of belief systems. Your characters have to change; there needs to be growth, and there needs to be a changing of minds. Secondly, know your tropes and when you've landed on one (or two), find a way to flip it on its ear. Do the unexpected. Surprise the editors. That will make you stand out. This advice works for single title authors as well, but especially for category.

Anna J. Stewart

CONFLICT IS the heat in your story, the friction that generates the momentum to keep your reader turning pages. Conflict is what keeps things interesting! But it can't be forced.

If you have twenty thousand words to go and suddenly your adorable lovebirds erupt into a Big Misunderstanding because you don't want to be short on word count, your readers will run away screaming.

Category romance readers are smart, and they know when they're being manipulated. Your conflict needs to flow beneath the plot and the characters, waiting to be tapped before the first chapter is written.

Seem extreme?

Every romance reader knows upon the introduction of the first trope what these characters are going to need to do in order to transform enough to be together. They show up craving certain flavors of conflict.

It's important to know enough about conflict to meet reader expectations, and enough about what's expected to throw in a surprise or two to keep things fresh. But more than that, a good writer is aware of not just conflict, but of the degree of conflict. Small conflicts make for fun banter. Giant conflicts make the wedge that threatens to drive our characters apart. Medium conflicts can be practice to overcome the larger ones.

Keeping the friction in balance is the difference between engaging a reader and frightening them away, and that's why it's important to identify and use the types of conflicts that appear naturally, using romance tropes.

Keep things lively—not irritating.

The Inside and the Outside

THERE ARE essentially two kinds of conflict: internal and external, the beast within and the wrecking balls of God without.

The important thing to remember about these conflicts is that they are not separate. In fact, in really well-written fiction, they work together to affect character transformation, which is the heart of romance and romantic fiction. But since good romance starts with character, the central conflict of the story has to start with character too. So that's where we'll start.

Internal Conflict: The Beast Within

ROMANCE TYPICALLY starts with characters in emotional, if not situational, stasis. Change arrives in the form of an inciting event. With category romance's shortened timeline, it's helpful if the inciting event *is* the other character. Their collision results in conflict as they struggle to change inwardly in order to accept the change that this other person makes in their lives. No matter what the plot tropes, it's this inward battle that makes up the characters' *internal conflict*.

Sources of internal conflict vary—and often they depend on the character itself. The list of character tropes is a place to start. The Tragic Past, the Orphan, Cinderella, the Sexual Butterfly, the Protector—each one of those characters obviously comes with their own baggage, and all of it is fighting the good fight in this poor character's soul.

Following are some basic examples of internal conflict, separated into three basic flavors: releasing, overcoming, and learning. If you want to spend a fun time plotting, look through the character trope list and try to figure out which characters are most likely to have which conflicts!

RELEASING	OVERCOMING	LEARNING
Bias	Fear	Self-control
Anger	Self-doubt	Confidence
Grudges	Self-protection	Mastery
Distrust	Apathy	Positvity
	Guilt	Forgiveness
	Obsession	Inclusiveness
	Personal flaws	

So many sources of internal conflict, right? But one of the most important things to remember in category romance is that much of the raging internal storm is going to be either incited or exacerbated by the other character. There isn't that much time for the internal conflict and the external conflict to be out of sync.

Romance is about transformation: two functional but incomplete humans meet and reshape each other until they become one working unit. The internal conflict needs to be part of the resistance to this change—the characters need to grow so they can fit together at the end.

But that doesn't mean that external factors don't have a say in what shape their puzzle pieces will take.

EXTERNAL CONFLICT: GOD'S WRECKED BALLS

THERE ARE a few basic types of external conflict. Like tropes, some of them can be renamed and reclassified according to what you are most comfortable with, but for the purposes of *this* little tome, they fall into these rough categories:

- Character vs. Character
- Character vs. Nature
- Character vs. Society
- Character vs. Forces (supernatural/divine/technological)
- Character vs. Destiny or Fate
- Character vs. Time

Any story will have at least one of these types of conflict, and some will blend several different flavors to generate maximum tension and drama.

The most important thing to remember about external conflict is that any *outside* conflict must affect the *internal* conflict the character is undergoing. I teach a class in conflict, and one of the activities I have my students do is break down books or movies into internal and external conflict. I've got two breakdowns here—one is the breakdown for the original *Beauty and the Beast*. The other is the breakdown for *Beauty and the Beast* if it was a category romance.

For each discussion of conflict, I'm going to ask just one question: *How does it further the romance?*

This is an all-important, all-consuming question—or it should be for a category romance writer—because in a good short-form romance, *every conflict needs to further the romance*.

In something larger or more mythic, it doesn't. The classic *Beauty and the Beast* is a bigger story, a more mythic archetype. Not every conflict in the story is about the two main characters. But it's interesting to note that in almost every retelling—particularly

Disney's—the conflicts that don't further the romance are cut. The movies needed to *compress* the story to make the conflicts tighter and more powerful. Keep that in mind as you read the chart for *Beauty and the Beast* the original versus *Beauty and the Beast* the category romance.

Remember, even if you don't make a chart like this and you are, like me, allergic to notebooks, the question you need to ask yourself whenever you throw friction into the mix is simple: *Does every conflict drive the romance?*

And of course, that begs the question: *How can I shave away conflicts to compress the romance?*

EXTERNAL CONFLICTS AND *BEAUTY AND THE BEAST*—THE ORIGINAL CLASSIC FAIRY TALE

CHARACTER VS. SOCIETY	
External	Beauty's family is financially ruined by a run of bad luck and is forced to retreat into the country, away from their luxurious lifestyle. Beauty's sisters are jealous of Beauty's good looks and kind nature. Beauty's sisters insist that Beauty needs to seek exile with the Beast instead of her father.
Internal	Beauty actually loves the simple farm life. Although her sisters aren't excited about the changes, she is fine with some books and the quiet, and this causes friction in the family.
How does this further the romance?	It sets up Beauty's character as an imaginative loner—but there are other ways to do this, and the sister's subplot isn't integral to the romance.
For category	She can be an imaginative loner without bitchy sisters, and Beauty's choice to take her father's place actually makes her a stronger person. Cut the sisters and the bitchery—Beauty only needs one family member to sacrifice herself for and to pull her away in the end.

CHARACTER VS. DIVINE/MAGIC	
External	The Beast has irritated a fairy or sorceress who has transformed him into a terrible creature.
Internal	The Beast's original self-hatred is exacerbated by his outward appearance and by its effect on the courtiers of his castle
How does this further the romance?	The Beast must overcome his self-hatred and defensiveness if he's going to learn to love Beauty and earn her love in return
For category	The fairy vendetta isn't really necessary for a compressed love story. The Beast can simply be a product of his own beastliness. Sometimes, when this trope is done in category, there is scarring and a tragic past. Sometimes the Beast is just a prick (with a tragic past). But having him atone to a force outside his natural control falls outside the set of romantic conflicts. So if you're looking to shorten your story, you might not want to use this conflict.

CHARACTER VS. NATURE	
External	What originally drove Beauty's father to the Beast's abode was an unseasonable storm
Internal	The snow and ice surrounding the castle (which, in the fairy tale, is warm and cozy) serves to emphasize the isolation Beauty feels when she takes her father's place.
How does this further the romance?	Two young people, all alone in an enchanted castle, with winter raging outside the boundaries? This is forced contact at its most romantic. The only way it could be better would be if the Beast looked good in a Speedo
For category	Forced Contact is the key trope to this plot. If there is no fortress of warmth in an unfriendly world, find another way to make sure these two characters can't get away from each other. (I myself chose an island paradise full of exotic animals who were once human in *Truth in the Dark*, but that's, well, another story.)

CHARACTER VS. DESTINY	
External	The Beast is doomed to remain a beast if he can't find somebody to love him for himself.
Internal	The Beast loves Beauty enough to let her go—and thus risks death from heartbreak in his beastly form because she has not yet professed her love for him.
How does this further the romance?	The Beast loves Beauty enough to sacrifice for her. By giving her the freedom to leave, he plants the seed in her heart that will bring her back.
For category	This theme can be present without the magic element, as long as there's some sort of ticking clock, which is a great thing for suspense. It would be very easy to give our Beauty a pressing reason to leave, and Beast's "doom" can simply be the loneliness of his own heart.

CHARACTER VS CHARACTER	
External	Beauty is at odds with her family because her sisters are jealous and want her out of the house. Beauty is at odds with the Beast because she has been compelled to stay in his lonely castle
Internal	The Beast is defensive because of his appearance and expects the worst of Beauty and her father, so he makes being around him even harder to bear.
How does this further the romance?	Beauty must learn to forgive the Beast and the Beast must learn to forgive himself. Both have to change inside to accept that the other's company gives them great joy.
For category	Again, lose the bitchy sisters and, depending on context and time allotment, the ailing father. Make Beauty's internal conflict compelling enough to pull her away, and her love of the Beast the drive that forces her to return.

CHARACTER VS. TIME	
External	When the Beast lets Beauty go visit her family (who has rediscovered good fortune and has moved from their rural setting to town), he is aware that if she doesn't return in a timely fashion, he shall die of loneliness.
Internal	Beauty, of course, loves her family and is torn between leaving them again and wanting badly to see her Beast again.
How does this further the romance?	It forces the Beast to learn the nature of sacrifice—which all lovers must learn—and it forces Beauty to choose her lover over her family, which is a universal signal of moving on to start a new family of two. The separation shows both lovers that they have done enough internal work to allow the other into their lives and heart.
For category	Transmute this conflict all you want, but definitely keep the ticking clock, which is one of the critical elements of a Forced Contact trope. Category romance thrives on a compressed timeline and on that suspenseful need for something to happen.

THIS CAN BE AN EXERCISE!

WHEN PLOTTING a category romance and wondering if you can fit all your conflict into one barrel, do a similar breakdown to the one above to see if your choice of conflicts contributes to the character vs. character transformation. But it's important to remember a couple of things first.

You are writing a compressed art form. Odds are good you won't have all six or seven conflicts at play in the pages of your story—in fact, you can probably only fit two or three into a 40-60K novel, including the internal conflicts. One of the first things I tell students when they ask how to keep their book within word count is to cut down on the number of conflicts any character endures. You need the internal conflict—always—and the character vs. character conflict—always—but a full seven-conflict book is going to be a lot longer than standard category length.

In order to keep those conflicts down, you will need to be aware of your world building. There will be a brief section on that later, but for now, keep in mind that while in a 120K work, there might be a lot of intrigue and subplots and several character arcs, in a 60K work, there are only the two romantic leads, a couple of buddies, maybe a bad guy. And that's it.

Do not forget that as the external conflict changes and moves toward resolution, the internal conflict must also change. The two conflicts play off each other. If they don't, the external conflict isn't doing its job. Going back to *Beauty and the Beast*, each external conflict leads to greater internal understanding.

Don't forget that if a conflict doesn't further the romance, it is unnecessary and needs to be trimmed.

WAIT—DID I SAY WORLD BUILDING?

YES, YES I did.

World building springs directly from story conflict, because the world establishes the stakes, scale, and scope of the tale you're telling.

Now you're probably thinking, *But if we're doing* Beauty and the Beast *as a category romance, do I really need to build a fantasy world? Unless I'm writing a paranormal category, who builds worlds?*

Short answer? *You* do.

World building isn't just coming up with rules for magic use or vampire hierarchies. *Every work of fiction builds a world.* In a contemporary romance, that world isn't made up of the fantastic—it's made up of the details you choose to show your reader to indicate what kind of story they can expect. World building isn't a setting—a setting is a time and a place. World building is the set of specific choices that affects everything from sources of conflict to available tropes. If an author doesn't make choices about whether the world in their book is a friendly place to lovers or a difficult place for everybody, the reader is going to be left filling in the blanks—and often not with what the author intended. You need to establish the rules of your world, or your intended conflict will be murky and your characters will be without substance.

If you are setting *Beauty and the Beast* in the middle of an urban city with the Beast as a corporate boss and Beauty being an adorable receptionist, you still need to build the world. Is this a world in which Beauty can make rent with one job? Is this a world in which health care is paid for? Is this a world in which Beauty has at least one fully functional parent and any true distress in their past has been dealt with in a healthy, responsible manner? Just by making those character choices, you have built a world with a slight fantasy edge. We all know those events don't often exist in gestalt with one another, but by making those choices, you have pared down the number of conflicts and focused on the narrative that advances the romantic plot.

That is world building.

If it helps, think of world building in a contemporary romance (or in a paranormal one, in truth) as a matter of *frame* and *lens*.

Frame is the small cross section of the world you're looking at. For a contemporary category romance, your frame is very tight indeed, with only the elements that affect your Main Characters inside it. For romantic suspense, your frame would be somewhat wider—big enough to see your lovers and a villain and their motivations. And for paranormal, it would need to be big enough for us to see whatever magic rules drive the paranormal world.

Lens is the filter you look through to see your characters and their conflict. Some lenses are, dare I say, rose-colored—they filter out the grit, the grime, the pain of everyday life. Some of them are hyperreal, like the lenses people use on the shooting range, so you can see a fly speck on a target two hundred meters away. Your lens determines what details you let people see inside the fictional bubble of your world.

With a category romance, you need to have a frame just big enough to fit the story inside the word count, and a lens that shows us the world in a way consistent with the category guidelines. So if your guidelines say they want a hero with some grit, use the hyperreal lens and show us this guy's scars and flaws. If they say they're selling a fantasy, you want everything to have the rosy glow of "too beautiful to care about the dirt." The best world building comes through character—what your characters see, your readers will see, so choose those details carefully.

There will be more about guidelines later. But for now, remember that every detail you choose to put to paper is building a world that your reader will get lost in, as well as the emotional state they'll be experiencing when your MCs embark on their adventure.

The same rules that apply to conflict also apply with frame, lens, and world building—*Does it further the romance?*

COMPRESSION

SO OBVIOUSLY conflict is important—and so is a character's reaction to it. But it's important to remember that a character's reaction is determined by their personality, as established from the beginning.

That's where our character tropes come in.

Your character's trope and personality will decide how the character reacts to external forces. Is your character quiet and introverted? Happy to spend time in a library or with her family? Well, that will make her happier in an isolated castle, but all the more resentful at being ripped away from her father and sisters. Did your Protector see his little brother abducted as a teenager? That will make loosening his control issues enough to see a romantic partner achieve some autonomy a whole lot more difficult. What about your poor Jaded Heart? Did she perhaps have a lover who abused her trust when she was most vulnerable? That will make trusting a wide-eyed young lover really difficult. Your Protector will resist protecting, your self-empowered Virgin will resist control, and your Cast-Iron Boss will resist gentleness—every trope has its frictional kryptonite, and it's up to you to find the equal and opposite trope that will create a super couple resistant to kryptonite because they complete and strengthen the weaknesses in the other.

Let's revisit conflict for a moment.

If we go back to our character tropes, you'll see that I put a list of sources for conflict right in that section. This list is important because while all books run on conflict, category romance *requires* compression.

Your character type, character trope, and character occupation all have to work together so you have more conflict per square inch. The character type, character occupation, and character trope need to produce conflict at their very source.

If we look at the sources of conflict, we can get an idea of how to maximize friction between characters and minimize world building and setup. If the reader expectations help us build the world, we can spare more words for the romance, and in a small space, that is a very good thing.

AGENDA

An agenda is more than just a list of items that needs to be done in a day. An agenda is a *priority* list. People who have conflicts over their priorities are people who have goals greater than themselves. People who are working for the environment, big business with a lot of employee buy-in, in education where student advocacy is important, or in social work where client advocacy is paramount. These characters are going to be *very* unyielding about their agendas—and very unbalanced in their personal lives. The Martyr, Sexual Butterfly, Cast-Iron Boss—these people aren't going to want to yield their priority of a greater good to a personal relationship of any sort—and they're not going to want to yield their agenda either.

BACKGROUND/EDUCATION

This is a fun source of conflict. Two characters may be compatible in every other way, but this basic, incontrovertible difference between two people can mask all of those similarities. What remains is a prickly discovery process rife with misunderstanding and sources for friction. Background and education are often *very* apparent in an occupation—a snowboarder with a high school diploma and his financier are going to have very little in common on the surface of things. A former ballet dancer and a police officer are another odd couple. The possibilities are endless, but the trope can be more than Opposites Attract. Ugly Duckling, Sexual Butterfly, the Virgin/Rake. Almost any trope in the list can be compressed by two opposing yet complementary backstories.

COMMUNICATION

Sometimes this can be as simple as a message gone awry—Romeo and Juliet would have lived to have lots of sex and babies if the damned Friar had been riding a racehorse instead of a donkey. But more often, communication is a source of conflict because people are just so damned bad at it. Falling in love is a tricky, vulnerable business, and explaining our feelings is hard. Human emotional defense mechanisms range from anger to tears to what appears to be cold indifference, and every lover has a different response to things that frighten or confuse them. Bad communication has ruined more than one relationship, and good communication is the root of all successful ones. This can be a source of conflict for almost every character and plot trope ever.

HIERARCHY/POWER IMBALANCE

This source of conflict usually depends on characters very driven by their jobs and jobs that insist on a pecking order. Law, law enforcement, the medical profession, behind the scenes in entertainment—any job that consumes a character's life but offers no security is going to inspire conflict here. Tropes that deal with a power imbalance—Enemies to Lovers, the Virgin and the Rake, Jaded Heart—are going to automatically deal with a hierarchy/power imbalance, so the character's occupations need to be chosen accordingly. The characters who clash on this level are going to have to be knocked out of their safety zone by the other character on a professional or occupational level. So their personalities need to be driven by their profession. Choose their profession carefully, because it's going to be referenced again and again and again.

PHILOSOPHY

A philosophy is the way we attack our agenda. Some people may have a very strong agenda and a very loosely codified philosophy, while some might have a very buttoned-down philosophy but a clear lack of priorities. The thing with a philosophy is that it's often only rigid if it's not challenged by real-life experience, and it's only truly out of control if people don't see the harm that can come from having no discipline whatsoever. Frankenstein's desire to look into what causes life and death was admirable—until he crossed the line and took no responsibility for what his philosophy had wrought. Philosophies require moderation, and they often go hand in hand with a character's occupation. Coaching, childcare, advocacy, social work, environmental work all demand a solid philosophy. This means they tend to bump up against their diametric opposites in the occupation area—industrialization, government, law enforcement, corporate culture. Very often, the Cast-Iron Boss, Beauty and the Beast, Jaded Heart, or even Sexual Butterfly tropes will find their way into a contest of philosophies.

PRECONCEIVED EXPECTATIONS

Let's face it, tropes *are* preconceptions. We are using reader expectations for how characters will clash to set up a story. We need to use *character* preconceptions to create conflict. What will someone of this education/background/agenda be *expected* to act like? How will these expectations be set upon their ear? Preconceptions work in in every trope on the roster. Just be aware of what they *are*. Look at your character one-sentence summary, look at their clashing agendas. How do we *expect* a person described this way to act? How can we surprise the reader and the other main character in a pleasant, sexy way?

TIMING/PLANS

Someone once said, "Life is what happens when you're busy making plans." Every romance begins when two people collide. They were bent on one path, and now they're ricocheting off each other. And with every hit, a little more of what was false or protective about each character is knocked away and it becomes impossible for these characters to resume the same path. They've changed shape. But have they changed enough to roll together? That's the suspense. This source of conflict is mined the most when the two characters are in different places in life. The May/July plot trope, the beginner and the pro in any occupation, the person who's about to realize a dream only to discover they've had a case of Mistaken Self-Identity all along.

Do a character's occupation and trope carry the same conflicts? That's compression. Does the plot trope work in conjunction with the occupation and the character trope to throw our characters together so they have to work shit out? That, too, is compression.

Now that we're talking about conflict, maybe, for the sake of this next exercise, go back and pick two character tropes—the Virgin Nanny and the Rake Boss, for example—and determine your sources of conflict. There should be one or two at the most. You can chart this out in your notebook. List the sources of conflict—Hierarchies, Agendas, Philosophies, Education/Background, Preconceptions, Timing/Plans, and Communication—on the left, and decide whether they're going to be an issue on the right. Or you can talk it through or write it through in a discussion that looks something like the one below.

In each area, determine if there's a place for conflict—there won't be in all of them—and if so, how can the conflict be compressed.

EXAMPLE: *THE VIRGIN MANNY*

AGENDA:

They both had sort of the same agenda—they wanted to make sure the Rake's nephew was being raised in a warm and loving environment. That was great! Both characters shared a goal and had something in common! It also provided conflict, though, under Plot/Character Trope, because our Virgin didn't want to engage in a relationship if it was going to hurt the little boy. He had to resolve his worries about what would happen to his charge if he decided to pursue his boss.

BACKGROUND/EDUCATION:

One was rich and the other was poor, but both had the same degree. Their differing economic backgrounds gave them some things to talk about, and it was a source of conflict at the beginning, but the education gave them some common ground and a solid place to build a relationship, even if they came about it from different directions. Conflict—resolved!

COMMUNICATION:

As mentioned before, this potential source of conflict was this couple's saving grace. Because they were both educated in the same thing. Communication was one of their strengths—and made it possible for them to overcome all of the other conflicts in their roster.

HIERARCHIES:

In the Virgin/Rake scenario, who has the power? Well, if you're writing *The Virgin Manny* (raises hand), the Rake has the power as the employer, but in their personal dynamic, both parties have equal choice of whether to initiate a relationship. So the occupation is one source of conflict in that area, but the character trope is another. That's a lot of conflict. If the characters hadn't shared some level-headedness and humor, it might have been too much to resolve in 55,000 words, so I took Communication out of the equation.

PHILOSOPHY:

One character believed in taking chances and the other character did not—as evidenced by their trope—but both characters believed family and kindness were important. That's one conflict off the board.

PRECONCEIVED EXPECTATIONS:

Our working-class character expected the wealthy character to abuse his power and try to seduce him. When the wealthy character instead presented him with complete autonomy and respect for his own agenda and life choices, the conflict was internal—our young Virgin had to decide whether to accept the terms of the relationship or reject the Rake character on the basis of preconceptions.

TIMING/PLANS:

These two characters had a ten-year age difference—which meant that Timing/Plans was one of the biggest conflicts of the book, not just between the two characters but between the young Virgin and himself. He wanted the relationship, but he had all these plans—he was fresh out of school and wanted to be a captain of industry. The older character was settling down with his nephew—and of course, he wanted a partner in life to join him.

But take note—the character traits, the occupations, and the trope created enough conflict to need very little plot machinery. The book didn't need any major misunderstandings; it didn't need a love triangle. In fact, the actual plot devices were very few. I do believe I added a thieving maid and a heroic fight for my own amusement, but for the most part the story was written just by the character tropes I chose at the very beginning. *That's* compression—making sure your characters and your tropes work together to drive the plot. If your characters simply react like real people tend to, two lovers working shit out will provide plenty of conflict for 55,000 words.

NOTEBOOK TIME: MAPPING CHARACTER CONFLICTS

NOW IT'S your turn. Look at the characters and character tropes you most want to write and decide where their sources of conflict intersect and create the friction that can drive the plot, and where their common ground can help save the relationship. Remember to look through your list and see where you can compress—where the occupation can serve the character trope, and where the character trope can add to the plot trope, and where things can work together to drive the same conflict in fewer words.

      This is set out as a chart, but it works just as well as the discussion presented above. Choose your format, but make sure you consider your sources of conflict—it all comes down to them.

SOURCE	CONFLICT	COMMON GROUND
Agenda Occupation Character Traits Plot/character trope		
Background Education Occupations Character Traits Plot/Character Trope		
Communication Occupations Character traits Plot/character trope		

SOURCE	CONFLICT	COMMON GROUND
Hierarchy/Power Balance Occupations Character traits Plot/character trope		
Philosophy Occupations Character traits Plot/character trope		
Preconceptions Occupations Character traits Plot/character trope		
Timing/Plans Occupations Character traits Plot/character trope		

Again, you may use this as a chart and fill it out for maximum conflict, or do what I did and simply talk it out to figure out what works best. And remember all of the variations different authors can throw into the same plot trope. Is your Rake hands-off as a parent and the Virgin a hovering nanny? Was one of them raised by flower children and the other one raised by wolves? Make sure the two characters clash on a couple of levels—but not all, and not none.

Go back to our concept of haiku. Every trope suggests its own set of conflicts. What else in the story works with those conflicts? Make sure you keep your powerful sources of conflict and, like in a haiku poem, trim all of the extra syllables to make things happen.

Remember, the clashes are the conflicts that drive the plot. The similarities are the common ground they'll build a relationship on. It's important.

By the same token, if *every* section you've created has characters going in the same direction, there is no book to write.

Conflict creates engagement. With conflict, there's always the *possibility* that two people perfectly suited for each other may not see the most obvious truth in front of them, and we *must* keep reading until we know for sure.

THE BELLAMY

SO WHAT happens, you may ask, when you put together two characters who have not one major thing in common? Not much. And that's a problem.

When I was writing out charts for my Archetype presentation, I used the Marvel Cinematic Universe and the DC canon as well. One of the things I noticed was that the characters who had the most chemistry—Steve Rogers and Tony Stark, for example, or Batman and Superman—were the ones who were compatible in more than one item on the list of potential conflicts. In fact, sometimes they shared *all but one* item on the sources of conflict list. It's just that that one item made them *really* pissed at each other.

The character couples who didn't share *any* of the items weren't really memorable. Very few people write fan fiction about Hawkeye and Thor—they don't have enough in common to interest us, or each other. In short, they had nothing to fight over.

It made me think. Having things in common is supposed to be a hallmark of a good relationship. Why would having a *really big* difference versus a bunch of smaller ones make such a difference on paper?

The conclusion I came to was something I called the "fixed tom effect." I was going to name this character "the Steve," after my girl kitty and supervisor of my home office, but it turns out that script writers have been calling this character "the Bellamy" for years. The Bellamy—named after Ralph Bellamy, a character actor from the thirties and forties who seemed to specialize in losing the girl to the other male lead in the movie—has become a trope in category romance who exists outside *of* and useful *to* the main romantic coupling. The Bellamy is the "other guy" or "platonic bestie." They're usually not a villain and are often perfectly compatible with our other main character. In fact, they may even be a past lover or a prospective one, but something about the two characters makes their relationship much happier platonic. Bellamy has been effectively neutered by the lack of friction or spark in the relationship. That doesn't mean they're not sequel bait—lots of Bellamys show up in a later book—it just means that in *this* romance, they're the neutral other.

Fiction has had some memorable Bellamys. Hermione Granger was Harry Potter's Bellamy, but she was the love of Ron Weasley's life. Colonel Fitzwilliam was charming and kind and great at banter, but even if he hadn't been all set to marry for money as a family obligation, he couldn't hold Elizabeth Bennet's attention as more than a friend. Frank Churchill was Emma's Bellamy—fun to flirt with, but on the whole, both of them needed somebody more serious and grounded to be the best person they could be.

Yes, sure, Ron and Hermione, Elizabeth and Darcy, and Emma and Mr. Knightley all fought like cats and dogs, but one of the things that makes characters—and people—fight like cats and dogs is that the things they argue about are things they *care* about. And by this reasoning, if two people have nothing in common, they have no emotional investment in the other person's opinion.

Even if it's only a plot of earth big enough to fit one toe from each character, there *must* be some common ground, or neither of them will care enough about the other to argue. So when you're putting together your two character tropes, make sure they have lots to fight about together. But also make sure they have lots to *care* about as well.

If we don't see them care about anything, we certainly won't care about *them*.

When the Plot Thickens, Add Salt, Pepper, Garlic, Chili Powder...

IF YOU'VE chosen your character tropes right, some of your plot tropes have already been written. We'll look at the plot tropes in the next chapter, but before we get there, it's important to remember that in order to make these two people transform enough to fall in love, the following two things are going to have to happen to that list of conflicts:

THING 1: THE CHARACTERS HAVE TO REFORM THEIR BELIEFS SO THEY MATCH UP IN AT LEAST ONE MORE PLACE THAN THEY DO AT THE BEGINNING.

So, SAY, if at the beginning, the only thing they have in common is that a child is at the top of their agenda, by the end of the story, they have to share at least one, if not more, sources of mutual investment. They will never make a relationship work if they don't have *more* common ground at the end than when they started.

Now this doesn't mean they have to change who they are completely, but it does mean they have to at least empathize with where the other person is coming from. Background is something we can't change, but education is. Characters who educate themselves in other people's points of view have affected a change in themselves that can help sustain a relationship. Hierarchies at work don't change, but understanding someone else's job can help both characters appreciate what the other one does.

Just recognize that while we start out hoping the characters clash in a couple of different places, by the end, they have to agree more than they disagree, or their relationship is going to be on very rocky ground, and that's not an effective HEA.

THING 2: THAT ONE THING THEY CARE ABOUT HAS TO BE PUT AT RISK.

ARE OUR two characters working to keep a family farm afloat? That farm needs to be one step away from foreclosure until our lovers learn to work together to save it. Are they both lawyers for opposing sides? Whatever they're fighting about needs to come close to being eliminated until they come to a compromise. Are they both musicians for a rock band? Not if they can't work together.

Whatever it is that binds these two people together needs to be threatened. Our characters need to see that they care for each other as much as or more than they care for their common cause.

But note—this does *not* mean we put children or even pets in danger in every book. The threat doesn't need to be physical, and it doesn't even need to be dire. Children are threatened by having someone they care about removed from their lives. Having the nanny leave because he can't stand the idea of working with a man or woman who doesn't love him is a *threat*. Having their family unit disrupted is a *threat*.

In *The Virgin Manny*, the thing threatened was the family unit the manny formed with the child's guardian and the child if he decided to move on to pursue the career he'd been working toward before he met his true love. On the one hand, it doesn't sound like a big threat, but on the other, to people in love who care about the child they're raising, this threat is *everything*.

The stakes should be high, but high doesn't mean life-threatening unless you're writing romantic suspense category. In basic contemporary romance a broken heart can be the be-all and end-all, the alpha and omega.

Because this is romance, and we want our hearts whole and happy at the end.

Now, as you put your plot tropes together and throw in God's wrecking balls to start the plot going, you need to remember: every conflict, every resolution needs to work toward furthering the romance. Part of that is the characters learning they can change, and part of that is the characters learning what matters. Hopefully, it's each other.

CHAPTER 4:

PLOT TROPES—THE TRAIN THAT KEEPS ON COMING

I was never conscious of writing category or single title or paperback or hardcover. You just have to tell the truest story you know.

Jennifer Crusie
All About Romance
October 2004

I STARTED with characters and character tropes for a reason: all stories start with characters, particularly all *romance* stories.

Characters start out in one place in their lives, they meet, and then they do things and feel things, and consequences ensue, and characters do and feel *other* things, and more consequences ensue, and finally, after lots of doing and feeling and consequences and ensuing, characters end up at a different place emotionally and physically than they were at the beginning.

Voilà—plot!

In a basic student handbook, a plot is defined as "a connected series of events." In genre fiction, that series of events has a different focus depending on the genre. In mystery or suspense, a plot is a connected series of events that leads to the resolution of the mystery. In fantasy, a plot is a connected series of events that is influenced by and has direct bearing on the world that is built within the story. In horror, a plot is a connected series of events of a grisly, frightening, or horrific nature in which a satisfactory resolution for the main characters is not a given.

And so on—there are a lot of genres to choose from.

Of course, genres may cross and merge, but in order to have a successful crossover—romance *and* suspense, fantasy *and* horror—elements of each genre need to be present and woven together.

In romance, the plot is the series of events that leads the characters through their transformation to the end, when they have changed enough to live together happily ever after.

A quick word about "happily ever after." If you ever want to see romance writers draw blood, drop those words casually and say "but it's not really necessary." And then run. Because romance writers take those words *very damned seriously*.

I personally have always believed that if it's *really* happy, it will transcend death—but here, for category romance, we're going to say that a Happily Ever After (HEA) extends for as long as the characters both shall live and leave it at that.

Part of a category romance is meeting reader expectations, and readers expect a happily ever after. Dick with their hopes in any other genre and any other format—on your own time, because most publishers like happy readers—but don't mess with this one.

Not even *I*, infamous killer of fictional vampires, horses, man-gods, and WWII soldiers, deny the importance of the Happily Ever After in a category romance.

But just because the ending is a foregone conclusion, that doesn't mean the ride to get there isn't a fun one. Our characters are interesting, and given that every character has his or her own trope or tropes, we know they have some growing to do before the end, and that's entertaining too. But constructing the plot—the series of events—that the characters travel through is its own challenge.

Remember, you have to pack an entire romantic adventure—character development, plot, everything—in a *very* limited number of words.

Cindy Dees, author of more than fifty category romances for Harlequin and a multiple RITA Award winner, says this about plot:

> *Everything has to work for you in a category romance. Setting, backstory, secondary characters, description—all of it has to pack a punch in the tight*

confines of a short novel. Which is to say, lazy writing won't cut it in category length.

Plot tropes are a way to shortcut much of the work that goes into constructing an interesting story with intriguing characters, without going overboard on the words. But in order to realize how to use your tropes, you need to understand how plot works.

FISH FREYTAG PYRAMID

SO, WHEN Damon was trying to convince me to write this book, one of the first things I said was "But I don't even know how to ask for rights—don't I need to license rights to talk about other people's ideas?"

"Like who?"

"Like the guy who came up with Frey's Pyramid."

"Gustav Frey*tag* died in 1895, sweetheart. He doesn't want your money."

"Oh, thank God. Okay. I might really do this."

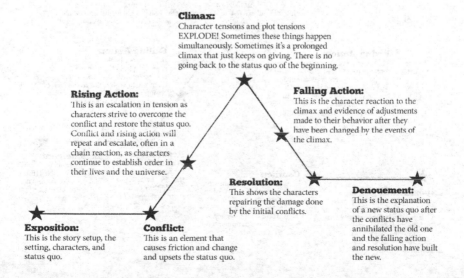

FREYTAG'S PYRAMID

Climax:
Character tensions and plot tensions EXPLODE! Sometimes these things happen simultaneously. Sometimes it's a prolonged climax that just keeps on giving. There is no going back to the status quo of the beginning.

Rising Action:
This is an escalation in tension as characters strive to overcome the conflict and restore the status quo. Conflict and rising action will repeat and escalate, often in a chain reaction, as characters continue to establish order in their lives and the universe.

Falling Action:
This is the character reaction to the climax and evidence of adjustments made to their behavior after they have been changed by the events of the climax.

Resolution:
This shows the characters repairing the damage done by the initial conflicts.

Denouement:
This is the explanation of a new status quo after the conflicts have annihilated the old one and the falling action and resolution have built the new.

Exposition:
This is the story setup, the setting, characters, and status quo.

Conflict:
This is an element that causes friction and change and upsets the status quo.

Before I knew about Freytag's Pyramid, I told students about "the heartbeat of literature," because there is an organic rise and fall, tension and release, to all good storytelling. Gustav Freytag, a German playwright and novelist, encapsulated this idea in what later literary types called Freytag's Pyramid, and it communicates one of the basic concepts of storytelling.

Now this pyramid structure works with about every plot known to man. It's an organic structure, a natural way to tell a story that keeps people's attention. But one thing that's important to note is that Freytag wasn't using this to map *character* tension—he was using it to map *audience* tension. As a category romance writer, you are using this concept as a tool to make your story suspenseful. As you're plotting your conflicts, your climax, your denouement make sure you're focusing on where the audience is going to be the most emotionally excited. Sure, one of your characters may be very sure they love the other, but will the other return those feelings? That the characters themselves know is immaterial. But is the *audience* hanging on the edge of its seat?

FREYTAG'S PYRAMID

Climax:
There's a whole chapter coming (snort!) about climax and how it doesn't always need a condom—*but*, in a category romance, physical intimacy must be part of the climactic resolution of all of the conflict. Even if your category guidelines insist on "sweet," fade-to-black sex scenes, there needs to be an expectation that these two characters will consummate their growing internal and external tensions physically. That being said, just because they both cry out each other's names in the moment of passion doesn't mean all the shit's been sorted.

Rising Action:
The rising action in a category romance must always escalate sexual tension. Very often category romances deal in a compressed timeline. One of the ways to make it believable that two people can fall in love in the course of a week or a month is that the sexual attraction is always visible, always present, and always rising.

Falling Action:
In a romance book, the MCs—after recovering from the climax—discover how their relationship has changed them as people. It is this recognition of change that makes it possible for their future together to be possible.

Conflict:
Every external conflict *must* impose internal conflict for the characters, whether it causes friction between them or inside them. There is no room for a storm that does nothing more than get them wet.

Resolution:
In a category romance, the resolution shows us that the characters can rebuild their own status quo together.

Denouement:
This can mean only one thing: a believable HEA. Show us two people who can live together happily ever after, forever and ever, amen.

Exposition:
The story and character setup *must* include both characters, *their* conflict, and the plot conflict that might keep their Happily Ever After in doubt. This is why category romance writers engage tropes—they give readers a shorthand for what to expect.

And as a writer of genre fiction—fiction that has expectations according to its focus, in this case romance—you should be aware that certain expectations happen with each stage of the pyramid that are specific only to *that particular genre or subgenre*. Often these expectations are unwritten; the publisher's guides will expect you to know what they are.

A rough approximation of the elements of literature rewritten for category romance is on page 72. As Cindy Dees said, you will see that these elements do double duty in this compressed form of literature.

It's a lot to do in 40-60K. And to that end, we employ plot tropes, and yes, some of those plot tropes suggest character tropes as well. Everything has to do double or triple duty. The more conflict you can give a reader in the fewest words, the more the reader will want to read to see how those people they love so much will fix that terrible situation they find themselves in so they can spend their time in love.

ALL ABOARD THE PLOT TRAIN

HAVE YOU ever seen a train in action? All the cars moving so smoothly it's like one sinuous metal snake?

That's how you need to think of plot construction. It's not so much an assembly of tropes plus conflict plus characters plus rising action plus climax equals resolution.

It's one long, polished, linked train that can be dissected into disparate parts but must function as a whole entity, all chugging toward Happily Ever After station.

So remember that when you're considering a list like this—a list of various plot bits that can be assembled into a story—they must be joined smoothly, so that when viewed from afar, the train looks like an entire beat. The conflict must flow smoothly from the characters and their tropes, and the plot tropes must come organically from the character interaction. The character interaction must produce more conflict, and that conflict must be resolved by the continuing interaction that follows. Sure, you as an author can see the individual cars as they're hooked up, but a reader can only see the big choo-choo and be excited about where it's going. Otherwise the magic of the train is lost.

Here are some—but by no means all—of the plot tropes you can use when assembling your category romance train. As with character tropes, these can do double duty, but I put them here because they have more to do with conflict than with personality or identity. I've organized these into categories that can—surprise—also double as tropes, because it's a broad world, and also, not a shock, some of these tropes fit into more than one category. They could also probably double as character tropes. Because characters drive plot, right?

So again, this is not the ultimate list of tropes. It's hardly a fraction. But I do have a word of warning if you're looking for tropes on your own.

As I was researching for this list, I found a lot of great resources that were happy, positive, and excited about romance. I also found a lot of resources that were bitter, nasty, and referred to the genre as "trashy" or "formulaic." As a whole, most of the resources that were negative listed tropes that are *no longer acceptable to almost any publisher out there*.

The resources that respect romance are the resources that read romance, love romance, and understand the modern romance reader. If you're buying roses off a fertilizer truck, don't be surprised if they smell bad. Use the resources that respect the things you love.

The following are some general thematic groupings with examples.

The Big Misunderstanding: Friend's Betrayal, Imagined
    Betrayal, Mistaken Identity, Getting Dumped, the
    Wrong Ring, the Other Twin
The Big Secret: Secret Baby, Lost Letters, Disguise,
    Masquerade, Secret Identity, Mistaken Identity,
    Fake Relationship/Engagement, Love Triangle
Enemies to Lovers: Blackmail, Opposites Attract, Forced
    Cooperation, Forced Contact, Class Warfare, Office
    Enemies, Homecoming, Revenge, More Alike Than
    Different, Suspicious Minds

Fairy-Tale Retelling: Cinderella, Beauty and the Beast, Snow White and the Seven Totally Platonic Roommates, Twelve Wild Ducks, Snow White/Rose Red, pretty much any beloved folktale

Fantasy/Wish Fulfillment: Time Travel, Royalty, Lost Heir, Soul Mate/Fated Lover, Lover Where Art Thou, Instant Baby, Instant Family, Fish Out of Water, Lover in Peril

First Love: Losing the V-card, Too Young/Stupid/ Stubborn, *Somebody* Doesn't Approve, Return to Hometown

Fling: Holiday Romance, One-Night-Stand-Who-Stayed, Amnesia, Accidental Pregnancy, Fake Engagement, Jilted at the Altar, Runaway Bride/Groom

Friends to Lovers: Childhood Friends to Adult Lovers, Childhood Crushes/Adult Platonic Friends, In Love Since Puberty, Sympathetic Shoulder, Not Quite Related, Office Romance, Unrequited Love, Widow, Common Cause, Love Triangle

Forbidden Love: Secret Romance, Family Feud, Secret Kink, Stepsiblings, Almost Kin, May/December, Polyamory, Dubious Consent, Hidden Engagement, the Worst Option, Stockholm Syndrome, Love Triangle

Forced Contact: Arranged Marriage, Accidental Pregnancy, Fake Engagement, Kidnapped, Marriage of Convenience, Amnesia, Matchmaker, Arranged Marriage, Mail Order Spouse, Almost Kin, Protector/ Bodyguard, Road Trip, Stranded, Suddenly Baby, Childcare Worker

Hands Off: Best Friend's Sibling, Sibling's Significant Other, May/December, Good Friend's Adult Child, Best Friend's Ex, Cougar/Sugar Daddy, Cyrano, Guardian/Ward, Matchmaker Matched, Employer/ Employee, Class Difference, Political Scandal, Widow, Childcare Worker

Hurt/Comfort: Wounded Warrior, Medical Care, Amnesia, Beauty and the Beast, Differently Abled, Pain is Gain, Trauma Survivor, Lover in Peril

Painful Past: Scars, Return to Hometown, Intense Regrets, Wrong Regrets, Ho with a Heart of Gold, Redemption, Orphan, Widow, Grief Grappling

Reunited Lovers: Second Chance, Working Together, Big Misunderstanding, Secret Baby, Forget the Fling, Big Secret, Lover in Peril, Homecoming, Love Triangle

Strong Hero/Heroine: Alpha/Badass, Billionaire, Sassy/ Bossypants, Heir, Law Enforcement/Military, Cowboys, Vigilantes, Bodyguard/Protector, Widow, Trauma Survivor

Time For a Change: Rut-Breaker, Fish Out of Water, New Horizons, Travel Transformation, Back to School, Learning the Ropes, New Job/School/Town/Look/ Skills

FROM ENGINE TO BAGGAGE CAR
(BUT NOT THE CABOOSE)

SO, GREAT. We've got some character tropes, we've got some plot tropes. Inspired yet?

Maybe, maybe not.

The creative process is a unique animal in each writer's mental zoo. Unfortunately, they are notoriously difficult to tame. There are other books out there besides mine that can help you outline a working novel, but there are some pluses to thinking about your book in terms of tropes.

The first is that conflict is essential to each story. If you choose your tropes carefully, you have built-in conflict by nature of the characters and plot you've chosen. If you make your plot tropes compatible with your character tropes, your conflict will be amplified.

The second is that category books need to be easily marketable not just to readers but to publishers. If you hop onto your train with no trope awareness, you are likely to get squashed by an editor or agent who can't figure out where your book will take them. Your tropes need to be front and center in your blurb, your synopsis, your character descriptions, and your pitch meetings. Thinking in terms of tropes helps you to be certain that your choices are compatible with the category line you are submitting to and are easily seen by the people who will be trying to edit, sell, and read your work.

The third is that you are writing a meticulously choreographed ballet. People usually know the story of the ballet before they even buy a ticket. Often, they can hum the music, just like most of you can hum bits of the *Nutcracker Suite* if someone asked you to. The audience goes to see the steps executed to perfection, the new imaginings of the costumes for the dancers, the grace and hope of the dance.

If you write a book without knowing what music and movements people expect, you are going to miss steps. So by all means, use the creative process that works for you. I'll admit, if people try to mess with what's in *my* head without my permission, I get cranky. But do make sure you walk onto the stage knowing what your dancers are doing. I'm watching a bunch of twelve-to-fifteen-year-olds learning pointe ballet as I type this. Their cores are developed, their thighs are developed, and they are doing some pretty impressive stretching and strength-building exercises before the music even starts. I'm damned sure if they hadn't been learning this art for the past eight years, they'd all be in a world of hurt. Make sure you start writing your category romance with your core muscles already built up to execute the steps.

Know your tropes, know your subgenres, know your plot structures, know your audience.

That being said, here are some thinking exercises that might allow you to stretch and strengthen, and might even help you choreograph your category dance.

NOTEBOOK TIME: MOMENT MODELING

THESE FIRST exercises can be used with either books or movies, because what we're looking for here is a moment, a feeling, a plot device that really flips our switch. We're going to look at the moment in terms of plot and character devices and see if we can recreate that *feeling*, that engagement or emotion, using different characters and a different plot—but getting the same warm fuzzies.

I have this laid out as strictly a thought exercise, but if you want to set it down in your notebook, that's fine too. The point here is to think carefully about what goes into creating the emotions that will tell your own unique story. If doing this helps you break the ice for your next work, that's wonderful. All I want you to do here is to be aware of what it is you love about your favorite stories of love.

For some of us, it's when we first hear about Jamie Fraser's ghost outside of Claire's house, before we even know who he is. That moment haunts us through *Outlander*—we want them so badly to live happily together. For some of us it's when Eve and Roarke are arguing about whether Eve should wear the obscenely large diamond he gave her as a gift, and just when we think her pride is going to make her walk out on him forever, she turns around and proclaims she'll do anything to stay— and he asks her if she thought he'd let her leave in the first place.

It doesn't matter which *moment* we've been trying to recreate in our writing, but it is time to look at the things that build up to that moment and see if we can find the magic ingredients to make moments of our own.

ONE OR TWO TWEAKS

LOOK AT the main characters of your favorite romance novel or movie and list the character tropes—all the character tropes—that they seem to fall into.

EXAMPLE: *WHILE YOU WERE SLEEPING*

>Lucy: Girl Next Door, Blue-Collar Worker, Unrealized Dreams, Orphan, Stuck in a Rut, Cinderella

>Jack: Boy Next Door, Blue-Collar Worker, Unrealized Dreams, Protector, Stuck in a Rut

Oh! Hey! Did we see that coming? These two characters actually have more in common than even they realized. Wait—now let's look at the plot tropes they employ.

- The Big Secret—Mistaken Identity
- Enemies to Lovers—Suspicious Minds
- More Alike Than Different
- Hands Off—Brother's Girl
- Fantasy/Wish Fulfillment—Amnesia

Excellent. Now that we know what building blocks this story uses, how can we tailor those building blocks for our own uses?

For each of these tropes employed by the movie, think of which circumstances you could change to help generate the same *feeling*, which of these tropes you'd like to keep, and which tropes you'd like to *add*.

CHARACTER TROPES—LUCY (SANDRA BULLOCK)

TROPE	DETAILS	KEEP OR CHANGE?
Girl Next Door	Single, struggling, charming, talks to self, spunky	KEEP
Blue-Collar Worker	Transit worker	CHANGE—If we make her work something in travel, we change the nature of the Stuck in a Rut trope and give her more agency.

TROPE	DETAILS	KEEP OR CHANGE?
Unrealized Dreams	College, family, travel	CHANGE—College, family, hometown
Orphan	Raised by single father who passed away	CHANGE—Raised by system after parents passed
Stuck in a Rut	Goes to work and dreams of Mr. Right	KEEP
Cinderella	Nobody notices her until she debuts in her Mistaken Identity by saving her "fiancé's" life.	CHANGE—Nobody notices her until she debuts in her Mistaken Identity by saving her *hero's child's* life.
Tragic Past	Lonely childhood, lost her only source of support as a young adult, lonely	CHANGE—Foster child, no permanent home, feels like she's constantly up in the air, isolated

CHARACTER TROPES—JACK (BILL PULLMAN):

TROPE	DETAILS	KEEP OR CHANGE?
Boy Next Door	Charming, self-aware, loves his quirky family	KEEP
Blue-Collar Worker	Works for his father's furniture reclamation business	CHANGE—Works road construction
Unrealized Dreams	Wants to handcraft furniture	CHANGE—Wants to handcraft dollhouses

TROPE	DETAILS	KEEP OR CHANGE?
Protector	Protects brother who is in a coma	CHANGE—Protects child who gets lost and is enchanted by rescuing MC
Stuck in a Rut	Works for father's company because it's easy, wants to start his own business	KEEP—Except he's working road construction for the same reason

As you can see, tweaking the details of the character tropes has resulted in adding a trope—Single Father—and our characters now have some common ground: they are now *both* in search of a family unit.

It has also resulted in revisions to our plot tropes.

- The Big Secret: Mistaken Identity (as a childcare or law-enforcement specialist, perhaps? Or we could lose this one entirely)
- Allies to Lovers: she helped save his child— they're on the same page now because of the Single Father trope
- Hands Off: Child's Caretaker
- Tragic Past
- Single Parent
- Fantasy/Wish Fulfillment—Instant Child, Instant Family

Compare this list to our first list of plot tropes—it's *totally different*. A couple of changes to our character tropes, and suddenly we are dealing with an entirely new story. We can still cast a very young Bill Pullman and Sandra Bullock—and they can be charming and adorable and fun to watch—but the shape of our story is completely different.

By adding a child, giving the first MC some freedom to run around the country, and giving Dad a slightly rougher job, we've kept the central dilemma—two lonely people who want a family unit—and changed the series of conflicts and potential interactions between them.

A couple of basic changes to the tropes, and this story becomes very different. And yet, as long as it ends with a Happily Ever After, it's still a story we want to tell.

EXERCISE B: EXCEPT EVERYTHING IS DIFFERENT

IN THIS exercise, we're going to pick a single trope—be it plot or character—and then build around it.

Let's go with one of my daughters' (plural!) favorite books, *To All the Boys I've Loved Before*, and the Fake Relationship trope.

The Fake Relationship can work a couple of ways. Either the two characters can pretend to have a relationship because they each have something to gain from it, or one character can offer the other character a bribe—or blackmail—to get their help. What matters is the two characters are put into Forced Contact, and while they're *pretending* to have a relationship, they become honest and vulnerable with each other, and a real relationship begins. The problem, of course, is that this relationship was started in falsehood. The characters can't be sure how much of their relationship is real, and they've both made themselves vulnerable. This is a classic example of Communication being the source of conflict, and the thing the characters have come to love most—their relationship—being put at risk.

In *To All the Boys I've Loved Before*, Lara Jean's little sister has sent the letters Lara Jean wrote to her most painful crushes *to the crushes themselves*. One of those crushes was her older sister's ex-boyfriend, Josh, so in an effort to convince him that she has no feelings for him, she asks the guy she crushed on in middle school, Peter, if they can fake a relationship instead.

Peter agrees to make his own ex jealous, and a Fake Relationship ensues.

This is a beautiful example of a Fake Relationship trope, but I've pared down a lot of the conflicts. If you read the book, there are interactions between Lara Jean and her father, her sisters, even Peter's ex, that all contribute to the plot as a whole—and are lovely in and of themselves—but that would muddy up a category romance.

So we love this book. We love the Fake Relationship trope, and we want to write a romance that makes us feel *just like that*—but we're writing for adults here, so we need it to go beyond high school, so the characters are of age and have a chance for an adult HEA. And we don't want to use Jenny Han's charming plot device with the letters, because she did it first, and it was brilliant. So what if…? What if…?

What if an up-and-coming business executive hits Send All on a highly suggestive mock email she'd written to a friend about her boss?

Oh no! Her boss knows she's got a crush on him! That's terrible! That's embarrassing! That's a sexual harassment suit waiting to happen!

So her friend—the one she was writing the email to in the first place—takes the hit and pretends she was writing that email to *him*. And now she and the guy she thought was her Bellamy have to pretend to be dating so the boss doesn't get suspicious. That's Forced Contact—and Friends to Lovers—in the same plot twist.

But it turns out the Bellamy is actually a lot more interesting than she thought, and as she grows more relaxed and happy in his presence, the boss starts to notice, and now *he* has the crush on *her*.

And now we have a Love Triangle.

It's just like *To All the Boys I've Loved Before*, right?

Except, as you saw, it's not. I picked that favorite plot trope, that favorite plot device, and then I invented new characters—and their characters evolved in different ways.

So…

Think of your favorite story and pick your favorite character trope and favorite plot trope from it.

Put those tropes in conjunction with other tropes to make an entirely different creature.

Keep that feeling that your favorite tropes gave you while creating your own original work.

It's pretty simple in the end. (No, it's really not. That's why we're professionals.)

INCOMPLETE

NOW I'LL be the first to admit my trope lists are incomplete, and their organization is a product of my own style of doing things. All lists are incomplete because stories and their elements *evolve*. But putting together these lists led me to think very carefully about how one type of trope leads to another. The Disguise trope can lead to the Forced Contact trope, which leads to Transformation, which leads to….

You get the picture.

Nothing in this book is locked in stone. The trope lists are a place to start, nothing more. If you're looking through the trope lists and find something you think doesn't belong, or belongs in another category—by all means, start your own trope list. Highlight your favorites, put them in your notebook, dream about them while you do the dishes, look at your favorite books and wonder how the author knew how to make that trope work just *so*.

Trope awareness isn't a product of reading a book about tropes and memorizing the lists. It's being aware of what motifs drive the stories that we love.

Be aware of the plot tropes you love most, and be on the lookout for new and creative ways to use them that involve characters you would love to talk to for as long as it takes to write a good book.

CHAPTER 5:

INTIMACY—NOT EVERY CLIMAX NEEDS A CONDOM

The sex scenes do sizzle a little hotter than usual....
There is genuine feeling between these two people and
they make a great couple. They're different, but equal.

Sarah Morgan
Bookish
January 17, 2014

WAY BACK in the eighties and nineties, when I read my first category romances, I remember telling my husband, "Oh, hey, wait, they're gonna have sex now. I'll stop reading when they're done."

"How do you know they're going to have sex now? Are they taking off their clothes?" We were very young in the eighties and nineties. Getting naked was high priority with us.

"No, but I'm on page 172. They usually have sex on page 176, call out 'I love you!' in the heat of passion, and then wrap up the book by page 187."

He didn't believe me, of course, but I'm pretty sure readers of category romance in that era could predict almost that exact sequence for 80 to 90 percent of the category books in those days. The other 10 to 20 percent fell into the Big Misunderstanding trope, in which the sex was about midway through the book, and then someone—usually the man—got all defensive and protective and said something super shitty that hurt the woman's feelings and made her feel used. Then we had to wait until the very end of the book when they both actually said what they meant and meant what they said and *maybe* got naked again before the curtain closed.

For anyone who opened *this* book and expected to see a breakdown telling you what has to happen by which page number and when the characters get to have the big bang, you will be sadly disappointed.

Romance structure doesn't work like that anymore. Relationships, social roles, and romantic expectations have evolved and books have kept pace.

Today's romance structure has less to do with what happens by what page count than it does with what tropes are meeting and exceeding reader's expectations. Back in the eighties and nineties, that sex scene at the end was important because if our girl *wasn't* a virgin, she likely wasn't exactly eyeballs-deep in healthy sexual relations either. They needed to cry out "I love you!" in the heat of passion so we all knew this wasn't just sex, that she'd never felt this way before, and they were going to get married at the end.

Climax achieved.

Sex means something different today, and modern romance has definitely kept up with the times.

For a while, I'm pretty sure romance was caught flat-footed. There was a scramble to find a "new" virginity, since many of our heroines were no longer hymenly challenged. Maybe she'd never had the Big O before, or maybe she'd never had a guy go down on her. Maybe she'd never actually tasted a penis and had always thought of it as "that thing that did the thing." I think, for a while, butt sex was the new virginity, and then gay romance got big and butt sex wasn't quite the big thing anymore—whatever. The point is that the quest for the new virginity had to stop before every heroine had to get spit-roasted on a yacht in front of a circus to be considered a woman.

And that was a good thing for category romance—in fact, it was a *great* thing, as romance groundbreakers like Cherry Adair, Rita Clay Estrada, Suzanne Brockmann, and Nora Roberts had been trying to show us for many years.

What the great writers—the ones who didn't cast perennial virgins and who used real sex words like "cock" and "fuck"—had been trying to tell us was that sex wasn't the be-all and end-all of a sexual relationship.

The "new virginity" wasn't what went where and how many had been there after all. The "new virginity" was that thing that *all* couples strive for, and sometimes it comes with massage oils and a visit to the sex store, and sometimes it comes with holding hands and actually having a conversation.

In fact, there are entire romance imprints built on the sex happening first and the long conversation happening later. After more sex, of course!

Because when it came down to it, we weren't looking for a sex act at all—we were looking for *intimacy*, and sometimes being naked with another person helped that and sometimes it got in the way, just like in real life. Very often, what all of the internal conflict and all of the external striving boils down to is the ability of the two main characters to be *emotionally* naked with each other—not merely physically naked.

Now, if you're going to use virginity or experience as part of your trope—and that's totally legitimate—of course making love is going to be part of the final outcome. In fact, if you're going to write *romance*, intimacy—even if it's a sweet kiss at the end with a promise for consummation after a wedding—is going to be part of the final outcome.

USING COMMUNICATION TO STRIP THE VEILS

NOW LET'S take a moment to talk about that sweet kiss at the end— or the banging wall sex in the middle or the slow seduction on the pages in between. Not all intimacy is the same.

For starters, in the guidelines section, you will see that there are category imprints that won't *let* the intimacy be the same. There really are some stories that fade to black as soon as the characters are in a room together, and some that have a sex scene but it's limited to one or two sentences. There are even category imprints that only imply that there will be sex, after the story, when there's a wedding ring on both fingers—and before you scoff, remember that many people consider *Pride and Prejudice* to be the most romantic story in the world, and the only place we so much as see Mr. Darcy's chest is in a movie that sort of shoehorned it in.

There are obviously ways to achieve intimacy without bare skin.

Intimacy can happen in a glance, the touch of a hand, a blush. Flirty banter can seem superficial at first, but if it turns serious, if one person says something perceptive and the mood grows soft, that's a moment of intimacy. An inside joke between two people can be intimate, the sharing of a memory—and it doesn't always have to be a painful one—can bring about closeness. Anything that strips away the veils that exist between two human beings and begins to reveal the naked soul behind it is considered intimacy, and one of the joys of a romance is watching those veils disappear one at a time, in a sort of emotional striptease.

Being physically naked and sexually engaged can be fun and exciting, but unless there's intimacy, it's about as romantic as scratching an itch, and generally, there's a progression to stripping the veils. Sure, there are tropes—Fling, Strangers in the Night—in which the lovers don't *know* each other well before they go skin to skin, but there is usually a moment of contact, of heart-to-heart understanding, that drives the breathless attraction.

The first veil is *recognition*. The lovers must recognize each other as specific individuals who have some sort of appeal. In Enemies to Lovers the recognition can be "Oh my God, that person drives me batshit crazy!" but it's still recognition. There is the realization and acknowledgment that this human being is special above all others.

The next veil is *emotional contact*. This can be as simple as eye contact—but sometimes time, space, and disability can interfere with that. Contact could be an unexpectedly vulnerable moment in an online chat. It could be the first time you hear the special timbre in a beloved's voice that you know is just for you.

After emotional contact, there's *communication*—and it can't be said often enough, communication needs to go both ways. However, both ways can mean one person speaking and the other listening. Communication can be banter, it can be the exchange of information;

it can be the telling of a joke. It can be one lover making a sound of pain and the other giving them a brief touch on the back of the hand. Communication is assertion and response. People talk about the "pathways" of communication all the time, but what they don't talk about is the implication of it. Every time emotion travels those pathways, people become more comfortable with who is on the other end.

And of course, once there's been communication, there's *revelation*. Even a lover without a deep dark secret may have secret corners that they're afraid other people will see. It's instinctive to hide the parts of ourselves we're afraid will be rejected. Once communication starts, our lovers are going to reveal themselves for their flaws, their strengths, and their quirks. Revelation is often a dramatic high in a romance novel—even if it's just the revelation that a heroine loathes housework, can't cook, or is actually really good at math.

And there they are, our two lovers, their emotional veils stripped away. They're naked—whether or not the clothes stay on. What's the next step?

Acceptance, of course. But think of it as an embrace—nude if you're in that sort of mood, but it can be a fully clothed embrace, if you'd rather. When people embrace, clothes shift, arms move, spines curve, hips cock; two people contort their entire bodies to hug and to, for a brief moment, become one. They accommodate the other's sharp angles and fill in empty spaces that the other didn't know they had. So beyond acceptance, there is "filling in"—or fulfillment. Two people become one. The ultimate physical metaphor for this can be sex, but for a truly emotionally satisfying ending, no sex is necessary.

But of course, remember your word count. All of these steps are necessary before we believe two characters can be emotionally attached enough to fall in love—but in a category romance, you don't have time to linger. In order to compress your timeline, to make the reader feel the intimate connection, it's important that you *don't concentrate on time*.

That recognition or acknowledgment that starts the romance needs to come very close to the beginning of the book. It's the spark of attraction, and while it doesn't necessarily need to be physical, within the first conversation or meeting, we need to see these two people acknowledge the other as someone of interest. The contact needs to come at their next meeting, and again, it doesn't need to be physical—it can, in fact be a clashing of ideas or establishing the sources of conflict and the rules of engagement. But it's contact, the second skirmish between two opponents who will only win the game if they end up together.

Communication needs to build. This is the rising action in Freytag's Pyramid. Every chance for communication needs to reinforce the idea that these two people are growing closer. Even if they're communicating by argument, the arguments need to get more intense and more personal. Communication needs to *escalate the tension,* one notch at a time.

The Revelation needs to hit hard. This is the emotional climax of the book, there is no other way to plot it. It can come before lovemaking or after it or even during—but the two characters must see each other for who they truly are when their emotions are most engaged.

Acceptance and fulfillment can come hard on each other's heels. "I accept who you are—you complete me!" is a perfectly awesome way to say "I love you!" As long as we know they'll be together at the end in the Happily Ever After, we have achieved climax.

When is Naughty Necessary?

But when sex is necessary, it's important to know at what level it's expected.

Usually your guidelines will tell you—and reviews of a category romance imprint often talk about sex and its explicitness by using flames, thermometers, or some other visual system as a guideline, usually on a scale of one to five. While the visual guide is nice, it's also important to learn the language. Some guideline language may include the following:

Sweet, mild, low heat, family-friendly, G-rated: Sweet romance means a few breathless kisses, some implied intimacy, but once the cardigan is unbuttoned, the lights go down and everything else is assumed. If the words *clean* or *Christian* are used, this means that the characters don't even have off-page sex until after they are married. I'm not a fan of that *clean* phraseology personally, because it implies other romance is "dirty," but if that's the romance you want to write, those are the words you want to look for.

Steamy, simmering, medium, PG-13: There is a lot of eye contact and pulse racing in this romance, a lot of simmer, some shivers coursing down spines and frissons of awareness. The sex, when it comes, can be on the page—but it's not necessarily explicit, and the vocabulary is suggestive but not graphic. If we're told a hero "maps his lover's skin like a monarch learning the lands he must give his life to," we can assume the lovemaking is thorough and intense, but we don't have to know what goes where. Sensuality takes the place of explicit hokeypokey. A few select details can make this romance *feel* more explicit than it is—the curve of someone's spine or the arch of their throat are actually fairly tame details—but in the context of sex, they prompt the imagination to do a whole lot more than the characters do on page. There is one sex scene, maybe two, in the course of a medium-heat book, and absolutely no reason for the sex to happen other than to further plot or character development.

Hot, spicy, or racy, R-rated: There should be some eye contact and pulse racing here too, but there should also be explicit language and specific body parts on page. We are *much* more cognizant of specific bodily reactions and what's doing what where. The sex acts themselves are not necessarily new—there's really only a few positions out there, otherwise it becomes human origami for shits and giggles—but we are very much in the moment as the characters experience them. Hot, spicy, or racy books have more explicit sex more frequently than medium-heat books, and the lovemaking can get quite intense—and realistic. This is not the place to talk about a man's erection. Feel perfectly free to say *cock*—but don't say it a lot. The sex in a hot, spicy, or R-rated book almost always builds plot and characterization—even while they're swinging from the chandeliers. Sometimes it's to show that our characters can play with their bodies, and sometimes it's to show trust—but there's almost always a story-specific reason for the sex scene.

Sizzling, scorching, graphic, NC-17: Reasonably explicit and fairly frequent sex scenes, with the sex words that will titillate and arouse. The sex isn't always to further the plot or the character here—sometimes it's just for its own joyful, playful, adventurous self. This isn't for the faint of heart—it's for people who embrace sex in all its fantastic animal earthiness and want to see it celebrated in big, bold thrusts of explicit words. There might be some light bondage in an explicit book, and there might be some toy play. There might be some edging or some positively filthy pillow talk. And there's definitely some fluids and a frank discussion of where they came from and what they taste like.

Erotic, kinky, very explicit, X-rated: So, everything that was in NC-17, but more and louder, with a close-up on genitalia and body fluids, lots of kink, lots of sex for sex's sake, and very often, one or two or five more people naked than you can expect in the other heat levels. In these stories, sexual exploration is central, and the emotional journey is mapped *by* the erotic contact. Because of the narrow focus on sexuality, writing at this heat level takes a specific skill set and verbal dexterity. Don't get me wrong, it's very possible to write a story that involves kink, extreme BDSM, and ménage or poly that is *not* explicit and X-rated, but the minute there are more than two people—or more than one sex toy—in that bed, this book will be labeled erotic romance. That is not a bad label, but on the whole, I don't think there are any category romance lines at this level of heat. I mean, if there are, let me know. I'm dying to write that Fake Boyfriend Threesome I've been dreaming about.

AND WHAT GOES WHERE EXACTLY?

WRITING LOVE scenes is really hard. Was I not supposed to say that? Imagining two people making love can feel unutterably invasive, even if these people have taken residence in your own head for months. The activities involve vulnerability, power, and personal boundaries in ways that make many people anxious and uncomfortable. I have no surefire cure or magic bullet to write a love scene, but I do have a couple of suggestions.

VISUALIZE

Close your eyes and imagine the people doing the thing. If you have to, break out your kids' action figures and have them do unspeakable things to each other to help get the blocking right. *Blocking* is a theater term for stage directions—remember you are telling people what to do so they will end up in the right place at the right time. Having a clear, concrete image will help you bring the scene to life.

DON'T GET TOO SPECIFIC

Don't obsess over right hand or left hand. "With one hand, he…, while with the other, he…" works just fine. Getting too specific can actually confuse people about what's going on. If we're focusing on what John's right hand is doing, we're actually forgetting about the kiss. You're not telling people how to assemble a stereo. Readers will *always* be more moved by the emotional impact than exhaustive chronicling of the boobs and bits.

SOME DETAILS ARE NOT NECESSARY

Nobody wants to know penis length in inches, the actual number of veins, saliva temperature, or the vaginal rainbow for a color-by-numbers painting. That transcends erotic and goes right to obsessive compulsive, and if I'm counting the veins on a guy's member, I'm not paying attention to whether he likes what I'm doing with my tongue. Remember, the relationship is the core of the love scene. Keep their attention where they will be moved.

LIKE IN REAL LIFE, PACING IS EVERYTHING

Love scenes need a pace that matches the emotional intensity. This doesn't mean that urgency goes super fast and exploration goes slow—it means that as the lovers' hearts forge a stronger connection by physical expression, the sentences get shorter, the author's words become more basic and more impactful, and the characters are often moved *beyond* words. Two articulate, bright characters clinging to each other in emotional aftermath is often way more moving—and far more romantic—than a bible full of discourse about how neither main character had ever come in rainbow colors before.

COMMUNICATION AND LAUGHTER ARE SEXY

I once wrote a romance that was supposed to be low heat, but I wrote out more explicit sex scenes and then cut them. Why? Because I needed to know what the characters *said* to each other when they were making love. What people say to each other changes their relationship—*communication* changes people, and laughter and kindness count as communication. Were these characters shy during foreplay? Confident during the act? More in love than ever at the end? These things were important to know, and the only way for me to do that was to write the sex scene as explicit as it needed to be, and then cut the explicitness and keep the communication.

COMPRESSION MEANS SEX SCENES STAY TIGHT AND DO DOUBLE DUTY

Category forces you to keep things focused. For the most part, sex should happen when it moves character and plot development. In some of the more graphic imprints, there's wriggle room for sex as play, but these books are short, and if you are going to devote time to a sex scene, the reader needs to see the characters changed in some way when it's over. These two characters may be very good at sex as a whole—they may be experienced, savvy, and have all of the confidence in the world—but sex with the person they're falling in love with is going to change the stakes, it's going to make sex special and a little bit scary. It goes hand in hand with that revelation and acceptance level of intimacy. If you're going to have a sex scene, we need the characters to see each other revealed for who they are.

WHEN THE CIRCUS CLOWNS GO HOME...

WITH ALL of those guidelines up there, it's easy to get lost in who does what to whom, how often, and with what equipment—but don't let heat levels and sex scenes fool you. Remember the ultimate goal in romance: emotional impact.

Always—*always*—the true striving, the true climax of the story, is when we realize that these characters have bared their hearts to each other, and their hearts have grown to beat as one. It's when we realize they can be completely emotionally vulnerable together, and they can face the world stronger because of it.

In fact, character is the crux and center of all intimacy. Going back to character is how writers of a thousand romances keep each scene fresh—no two characters make love the same way. Going back to character is how a new writer can start that first intimacy scene, because the two characters cannot actually grow if they do not somehow grow closer to each other.

The external, story-centered climax can come earlier or later—it depends on the story you're telling. If you're writing romantic suspense, I've got to say, there's nothing sexier than two people revealing their deep love for one another before grabbing a weapon and venturing into a firefight they don't think they can win (but somehow do). But then, the "Oh my God, I'm so glad we survived, but I was so afraid I couldn't tell you that I loved you!" is also surprisingly effective.

Sometimes the external climax is just as simple as "I got a job, I'm settling down here in this town you adore, please can we date before we eventually have babies."

> But the internal climax—the "I have been soul-strippingly naked in front of another person and they with me, and we can begin our lives together!"—absolutely has to be met by the end of a category romance.
>
> Let's be honest—it's sort of the entire reason your readers show up in the first place.
>
> Resolve the external conflicts so your two characters can be together physically in the world.
>
> Resolve the internal conflicts so your two characters can be together intimately in their hearts.

Those are the climaxes readers want—*need*—in order to find the book has satisfied them emotionally. That's the kick-back, smoke-a-cigarette, raid-the-fridge, post-emotional-coitus that puts a smile on everybody's face, and it's a lot harder than a bang and some awkward shouting during the Big O.

And remember, your denouement comes down to three little words. Not *I love you*—we should have gotten those earlier, during the emotional climax. No, your falling action, your denouement, comes down to Happily. Ever. After. It can be a page of epilogue, it can be a final chapter, it can be a marriage proposal we've seen coming since the emotional climax—but we need to know these two people aren't going anywhere when the curtain closes. We need to know they've made promises that they'll damned well keep. Emotional intimacy.

Happily Ever After.

If people complain about a category romance's formulaic qualities to you, remember that the two things people want at the end of that book are the same two things we want from our everyday lives.

It's classic because it works on all levels. And it makes us damned happy when it does.

CHAPTER 6:

GUIDELINES—PLAY BY THOSE RULES

It's important as a new writer to do two things. The first is to succeed at completing a manuscript. This means you sit down and write an entire book from page one/chapter one to "the end" on page 250 or 300 or 400 or 500. Often, to prove to herself that she can do it, a writer needs to write exactly what she wants to write—which sometimes isn't what the publishers want to publish.

But after you've proven to yourself that you can write a complete book, then it's time to focus and to write not just any book, but a specific type of book. Decide what it is before you start to write—and do research! If you want to write for Silhouette Desire, then read 100 Desires. That's the best way to learn exactly what types and styles of stories the editors are looking for.

Suzanne Brockmann
All About Romance
February 19, 2001

IF YOU Google the links to the Harlequin, Entangled, Dreamspun Desires, Tule Publishing, Hallmark, or Carina Press publishing pages, you will eventually find yourself on category publisher submissions pages, which list *many* imprints, plus guidelines for each.

Some of the imprints are "sweet" romance, with fade-to-black sex scenes or no sex at all. Some of the imprints are "bring out the trapeze and scented oils that make you make that noise" hot, and are about as explicit as you can get without an X-rating and a brown paper wrapper to sneak it out of the grocery store.

Some of them are romantic suspense, some of them are paranormal, and some of them may even include cowboys—but you have to read the guidelines to know.

Now, some people may read the guidelines and bristle: "Well, *my* romance is going to be *different*. I'm going to write characters that *I* want to write, and it's going to be as long as it needs to be, and my climax is going to come when I'm damned good and ready!"

Good for you! Write that romance! Be that trailblazer! I'm sure it will be splendid. Just don't submit it to that imprint's acquisition team if it doesn't meet their guidelines.

If you are submitting to Harlequin Dare and they ask for explicit sex scenes (and they do!), but you're more comfortable writing sweet, behind-closed-doors implied sex scenes? Find a different imprint. If you're submitting aliens and this publisher doesn't take aliens? Find one that has a *Roswell* imprint and go for it! Have you written in first person and your imprint only takes third? Well, either revise that manuscript or go shopping elsewhere.

The selling point of category romance is that it *meets expectations*. The secret to breakout category is that it *exceeds expectations* as well.

Find an imprint that you like to read—and if you haven't read any of them, *do*. I cannot be*lieve* how many people think they'll just whip off a category romance and submit it for kicks and profit when they haven't read one since they stole it from their grandmother's closet in the fifth grade. Or, worse, they've never read one at all.

Think about all the reasons you love that romance. Think about the things it did to your endorphin levels when you got to your favorite parts.

Think about the tropes that made your heart sing, the Happily Ever Afters that you can't get out of your head.

Think of new things to do with those tropes—things you haven't seen or haven't seen enough of.

Think about what you will do to make the tried and true into brand-new and you.

The branding of the imprint you're submitting to will dictate how you must brand this specific book. Otherwise, you have not met your editor's expectations and you won't meet your readers'. Besides—if you don't meet your acquiring editor's expectations, it's not like your book is going to get published for readers anyway.

Now, I have written plenty of out-of-the-box romances. My publisher expects them from me by now—in fact, my publisher's common question upon submission is "Will I need vodka, kittens, or cookies?"

My usual answer is "All three."

But my acquiring editors *never* have to ask that question when I'm submitting a precontracted book for my publisher's category imprint. I know my job. I'm a professional, and I submit the tropes we've discussed, with the word count I've been assigned, with the voice and vibe my readers expect from me, and I'm thrilled to do it. I've done my job, I hope. I've made people happy.

Your publisher's guidelines for their category lines are sacrosanct. Even self-published categories must keep their promises to the reader. That doesn't mean you can't be new and fresh, but it does mean you can't write cowboys for a vampire imprint and you shouldn't write drug-addicted porn stars when your category editor is looking for mannies. Sure, you can push the envelope within your guidelines—or even push the guidelines themselves, after you've been published a while and you have a good rapport with your editor and you know what to ask for and why it's important.

But I've always said that I wouldn't write where angels feared to tread if the angels had put up better signs. Category romance is the one place where the signs are written about as clearly as they can be. It is the submitting author's responsibility to read those signs and hope for the mercy of their acquiring angels.

What if your acquiring angel suggests a few changes and a resubmit? That depends. I've seen a lot of unpublished authors stick their noses in the air and say, "But I wanted to keep the integrity of the work!" I haven't seen many *published* authors do this, however. So before you even start your category romance, when it's still in the planning stages, look up those guidelines and commit yourself to upholding them with joy, wit, and grace. That's your challenge; that's your *job*.

GUIDING THE WAY

THE FOLLOWING is a guideline synopsis from a fictional category line I made up myself. All of the basic questions, challenges, and wisdom necessary to score a contract are baked right into this deceptively short explanation if you unpack the cues and clues. Let's dig a little deeper, shall we?

ANGEL'S TREAD CATEGORY LINE—60,000 (1)

Sexy. Passionate. Bold.

Angel's Tread stories push the boundaries of sexual explicitness while keeping the focus on the developing romantic relationship. Come meet the sexiest men alive! (2)

Key Elements

- The heat level is explicit and graphic. The hero and heroine have a powerful sexual and emotional connection. (3)
- We're looking for authors who have a distinct, memorable voice and write stories with a high level of sexual tension as well as graphic sex. (4)
- We want to read the ultimate alpha hero of all of your sexual fantasies! While billionaires, CEOs, and other successful, affluent men are welcome, we are also open to grittier heroes and antiheroes—military men, spies, and bodyguards. (5)
- Heroines are empowered, fun, and fearless women who don't necessarily need a man in their lives. Having a man is her choice... and she chooses to please herself! Strong heroines are a signature of this series, and their boldness and independence are every bit as important as the character of the alpha male. (6)
- Stories must be contemporary with an edge of sexual fantasy. Readers should be swept away to a world in which

real-world obstacles and challenges can be overcome in the face of love. (7)

- The setting can either be metropolitan (Paris, London, New York, LA, Sydney, Rome) or glamorous (the Amalfi Coast, New Zealand, Hawaii, the Caribbean). (8) The setting alone doesn't make the story sexy, but it certainly helps!
- We are only open to third-person POV. There should be a balance of POV between the hero and heroine. (9)
- A word count of 60,000 means stories must be fast-paced and plot-driven, but there is some time for introspection. (10)

We are open to many different story types and are especially considering law enforcement (police, FBI, etc.) and mercenary romances. We are not looking for western-themed, sports, small-town romances, paranormal, aliens, or historicals. (11)

These are sexy contemporary romances and we're not accepting erotica or erotic romance. We are not interested in BDSM (light bondage is acceptable), ménage, age play, bestiality, incest, or rape. (12) Each manuscript will be evaluated on how the subject matter is handled.

Submissions are being accepted in all three of our editorial offices. For more information, please contact: (13)

Gretchen Thomas, Executive Editor, Tallahassee

Halifax Trent, Senior Editor, New York

Janice Fast, Senior Editor, Australia

LET'S LOOK AT THESE GUIDELINES BY THE NUMBERS:

1. Word count: One of the reasons any mass-market publisher is able to give their authors such a huge distribution is that they print off a big whack of paperback books at a time. In order to do this, the length of the manuscript is *sacrosanct*. *A book of 50,000 words* means it's 45-50K long. Anything more or less will affect the spacing, the font size, and the page count. When you are dealing in publishing batches of more than 10,000, a significant deviation will affect the bottom line because word count changes the size, shape, and literal

amount of paper required to manufacture and distribute your masterpiece. That's why this number is inflexible. It has nothing to do with the quality of the manuscript. It has to do with getting this story into as many hands as possible as cheaply and efficiently as possible.

2. Heat level: This affects mass distribution. Some stores deliberately avoid stocking certain heat levels for corporate reasons. Readers pick up a category romance to stay in their comfort zone. If they're comfortable with the big sex words and hot banging wild animal sex over a desk in front of a window, they will pick up a book that signals that level of explicitness is included. Remember, this guideline isn't there to stifle a writer's creativity, it's there to make sure as many stores and people as possible buy the book because they are looking for branding that indicates this book is in their comfort level.

3. Emotional connection: Besides the words *graphic sex*, the other phrase to pay attention to here is *strong emotional connection*. The difference between porn and romance is the emotional connection—this specific phrasing tells us that the characters need to feel strongly about each other. You can probably use graphic sex words, and your hero and heroine can have robust, healthy sex lives, but they need to feel something powerful that differentiates their story as a *romance* and not erotica.

4. Sexual tension: This means that as explicit as the sex may be, we need to feel the simmer, the attraction between these characters when they're trapped in an elevator or when they're discussing their taxes. We're looking for a *connection* and a level of emotional intimacy here. This is not the place for your noir detective hero whose every line needs to be interpreted to see the connection. We need to be *shown*. The emotional voice here needs to be sultry and sizzling, not understated and dry.

5. Heroes: Alpha heroes, grittier heroes, antiheroes—this is saying that our hero doesn't need to be a sweet guy. In fact, for this line, we're looking for someone rough around the edges, possibly someone who has made mistakes and is seeking redemption.

This can be your real-world "asshole" who is actually a good bet as a husband because nobody is going to hurt his lover. Nobody. If this said "everyday heroes," we'd be looking for teachers and mentors. But this series wants characters used to giving orders and not playing by the rules.

6. Heroines: "Bold heroines" can masturbate. They can give orders. They don't care if people are offended. And they may love and appreciate sex, but finding a mate is not the be-all end-all of their lives. This doesn't mean that they're bitches—although they can be. It just means that they're unapologetically powerful. This is *not* the place for a Virgin/Rake story. It's *not* the place for a Sexual Butterfly or a Boy/Girl Next Door—that sort of sexual realization has already happened for these characters.

7. Subgenre: The key words here are "contemporary" and "sexual fantasy." There are no vampires here, no time traveling, no cowboys. There is just enough world building for us to believe that the glamorous, powerful, and sexy people on the page could actually invite us to dinner and it would be fabulous. But other than that, they live in the real world. There can be some grit, there can be some pain, but the fantasy is that a true emotional connection can carry us beyond all of that, and that real people in this world can be happy in the end.

8. Setting: "The setting alone doesn't make a sexy story, but sometimes it helps." This is not the place for your backyard. This is the place for some glamour, for some fantasy. A weekend in New York means a hotel in Manhattan, not visiting a cousin in Queens. This line is obviously fantasy-driven—you need to give your reader their favorite dream. If only their lives were in Paris, everything would be fine.

9. Point of view: The POV is important here in that it's stressed as "balanced." This is not the place for a first person with *only* one person's perspective. As I said in the character chapter, in a category romance, both characters must show growth. This line is insisting that both perspectives bring specific character development to the story.

10. Pace: "Fast-paced" and "plot-driven"—this is not a place for internal angsting or the delicate dance of sensibilities, as the words "character-driven" would indicate. These people meet, they connect, they bang, they grow, they bang some more, they solve their external conflict, and they figure out how to be together. Also—remember that external conflict chart you had to fill out a few chapters back? "Plot-driven" indicates that more than one external plot point needs to be introduced and covered.

11. Boundaries: See all those things we're not considering? Do not submit them. Look instead for other category lines that *are* considering those subgenres and tropes and submit to them. And if you don't find a category romance line that wants to publish what you want to write, it may be time to rethink what you want to write or how you want to publish. That doesn't mean your story isn't good. It just means that these stories are written for a specific audience and that might not be your thing. As someone who has written more than one niche story, I know full well that it's not productive to howl at the moon. The moon doesn't hear you. Prepare your manuscript with your gatekeepers in mind or be prepared to adjust your publishing goals.

12. Deal-breakers: Oh dear God. Please. Just don't. Whatever your weirdest kink is, a corporately driven publisher isn't the venue. Mass-market category romances do well because they appeal to as many people as possible and because each imprint caters to a specific taste. There are places online for niche kink—as long as it's *legal!*—but a category imprint is not one of them.

13. Editors: Pay attention to the specific editors you are submitting to. Look up their bios if they're offered on the main page and see if they have particular interests or wish lists at the moment. Address your manuscript to a specific editor as indicated by the guidelines. If your vampire/cowboy BDSM ends up in the hands of an editor who only does sweet Amish romance, *this is a bad thing*. And

the publisher has gone to lengths to make sure that doesn't happen by listing your contact editors in this space.

SO, ABOUT THOSE GUIDELINES

SO, WE'VE been doing fun notebook and creative exercises to help us focus on trope awareness and creating compressed category language.

Put the notebook away for a moment and scan through some guideline links. Do you see anything there you want to write?

Do you see anything there that sparks a plot idea? Do you see a line there you've loved to read for years and want to be a part of?

In category romance, you are writing for a specific audience, and they know what they want. That's why the guidelines are specific, and that's why tropes are so important. When you write your book, have your audience and your guidelines in mind. You are not freestyling here—you are writing a very specific story.

But that doesn't mean it's not a huge adrenaline rush to put that story together.

Think about the tropes we've discussed and about rising action and conflict and climax. Look at those guidelines again, with an eye to the *fun* you'll have coloring inside those lines.

Now start planning your romance, making sure to tick off each box in the guidelines as you do. Remember your strong word choices, your boldly printed characters, the way to make the story you and not just tried and true.

And keep writing.

AND ABOUT WRITING...

NOT GONNA lie here. Actually writing the book is a pain in the ass. It will haunt your dreams and consume you. You will be sitting in a quiet room with your significant other and they will say, "Who are you talking to?"

"Hush! They've almost had their argument and they're about to knock boots!"

You have voluntarily immersed yourself in a fantasy world, and you can only exit when you're done. That being said, the actual *mechanics* of assembling all of your daydreaming into a compact novel will vary.

I have a couple of suggestions for people who are feeling overwhelmed—ways to start actually writing the book of your dreams. Feel free to try any of these out, but remember, this is definitely not a one-size-fits-all process. Find the drafting technique that works best for you.

FREYTAG'S PYRAMID

This involves a simple sketch before you start writing. In your notebook, sketch out Freytag's Pyramid, as shown on page 62, and for each spot on the pyramid, figure out what your characters are doing. This will force you to process your status quo, your incident, your external conflicts, your external climax, your character climax, and your new normal in the very end. It is essentially a plot map that can help guide you from scene to scene, showing how the tension will escalate as you go. That way, every time you sit down to write, you know where your people are going and how this book is going to end. The double pyramid works best. Build the pyramid twice—once for the external conflicts and once for internal. This is particularly helpful if you are writing romantic suspense—the characters' internal arcs need to be just as suspenseful and exciting as the things that happen to them externally, and the internal and the external need to be connected.

POST-ITS

I would suggest you start by writing out your one-sentence character summary, your character tropes, and the plot tropes you want to use and either put them on Post-its and put those Post-its in a place of honor, or write them out on a sheet of paper and thumbtack that to a wall. Then write—in brief—one sentence for each scene you want to write. *They meet in an elevator and banter*, *We see MC1 needs MC2's services*, *Visit to MC2's office*, and so forth, until the entire plot is mapped out, Post-it to Post-it. Extra points for putting them in a shape of a pyramid and matching the action to the shape. After you've done this once or twice, you will probably get a feeling for how many words you write per Post-it, so it's a nice way to control your word count before the book is even started.

MAP YOUR ELEMENTS

This is a good one for the notebook. List everything by element—character descriptions, character tropes, internal and external conflicts, plot tropes, climax, the shape of the HEA—and then start writing with the goal of covering all those things by the end of the book. Blake Snyder's Beat Sheets—found in his book *Save the Cat!*—have proven effective for many category writers if this sounds like your cup of tea.

WORD COUNT STRUCTURE

This one demands you look at your guidelines first, then break your book up by word count along the lines of Freytag's Pyramid. There are a lot of books that can give you a breakdown for this—and a better breakdown than mine, I'll be frank. *On Writing Romance* by Leigh Michaels has romance writers sharing their best tricks, and *Romancing the Beat* by Gwen Hayes introduces writers to a step-by-step process. Both books are excellent and cover this topic on a much deeper level. A *very short* breakdown of a 50K manuscript—with moderate to extreme heat level and contemporary world building only—might look something like this:

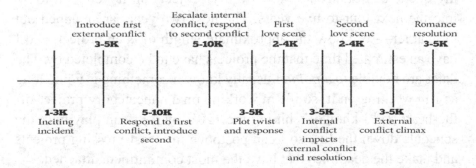

Inciting incident—: 1-3K
Introducing first external conflict: 3-5K
Respond to first conflict, introduce second: 5-10K
Escalate internal conflict, respond to second conflict: 5-10K
Plot twist and response: 3-5K
First love scene: 2-4K
Internal conflict impacts external conflict and resolution: 3-5K
Second love scene: 2-4K
External conflict climax: 3-5K
Romance resolution: 3-5K

If you're breaking your book up by word count, you might want to have already written out your inciting incident, external and internal conflicts, etc. on a Post-it or a pyramid or in a notebook. But some people prefer to fly by the seat of their pants.

BUT AMY DOES IT THIS WAY

I FEEL a little naked writing this section, because there's actually very little to say. I've already confessed to not using a notebook, and now I'm going to confess to having very little method to my madness. It's humbling.

I am far enough into the publishing process that my publisher has a list of projects that I've pretty much promised to fulfill. My editor and I playfully call it the queue of insanity. At the moment, my queue of insanity has about thirty projects on it—enough to go into the next four to five years. The next two years are mapped out by quarter—we know the approximate length of each project, and I have an estimated time that the projects have to be completed by. The dates are flexible *to a point*. I usually know if something is going long as I'm working on it, so if I'm working on a noncategory project-of-the-heart and I know it's hitting the 120K mark, I can play with the schedule down the line so I can postpone my least-pressing projects and make the deadlines that have the most commitment attached.

My category romances are the most vital because they are mass produced and scheduled far in advance of release. I can't miss those deadlines or I lose my slot, so I work my other projects around them.

Because I have such a long lead time, I have played with these characters in my head for *months*. I have imagined their conversations, I have made mental lists of their character traits and conflicts. By the time I sit down to write, these people aren't a list in my notebook— they've been my constant companions for a while. While I'm walking the dogs, driving to pick up the kids, washing the dishes, these people are hashing out their love lives in my head.

By the time I sit down to write, I know where they are at the beginning of the story, where they have to be in the middle, and I've got a pretty good idea how they're going to make their broken parts match so they fix each other.

I don't know everything about how this story is going to end, but I know enough.

Usually I know *just* enough to hunker down and write them, from beginning to end, at a rate of between 2-3,000 words a night, unless an edit lands on my desk. And I keep writing. And when I hit a spot where I don't know how to get from point A to point B, I get up and get a drink of water and figure it out. Then I sit back down and keep writing. And sometimes their conversations take fun turns, and sometimes their plots find a place to go organically that I had not planned on, and I keep writing. Very often I have to leave behind something I'd planned for my characters to do in favor of something they actually need to do in order to fulfill the trope and conflict expectations I set down at the beginning of the book. Plot and character tropes feel very organic to me—I just have a pressing need to see them through.

And still, I keep writing until I get to the end.

It's not very scientific, I know, and it doesn't lend itself to a treatise on how to draft a manuscript. But the takeaway here for someone who is beginning is that I've thought about plot tropes and character tropes and the inevitable human results of conflict and audience expectations for *months* before I break paper on my basic Word program. No matter what your favorite approach to drafting a manuscript may be, you need to concede that it's going to take some time in your head or in your notebook or on your computer to get your category romance to the place it needs to be. You will need to imagine and discard scenarios, and envision and table quirky subcharacters.

Setting out tropes and conflicts at the beginning of the story sets out a promise to your audience. If you tell someone in chapter one that *this* is going to explode, and they don't see fireworks by the end of the book, your readership is going to be *very* unhappy. Whatever in-script plans you need to cancel—quirky secondary characters, amusing subplots, funny banter—to get to that fireworks display by the end of fifty thousand words is the kind of self-editing you need to do in your category romance.

You will need to revise your own expectations based on what your characters absolutely need to do to fulfill audience expectations. It's inevitable.

It's the writing process for someone writing within a limited word count—and it takes commitment.

AFTER "THE END"

WHEN YOU'RE *done with your book*, revisit the guidelines again. Ask yourself, "Does this really fit the original call for submission, or am I squidging in some places in the hopes that they'll just think I'm cute?"

And be honest.

If your Law Enforcement Officer turned into a Cowboy overnight and your chosen imprint doesn't *take* Cowboys, it's time to do some reevaluation. You can either A) go back and flog that Cowboy until he takes off the hat and puts on a damned badge, or B) find a home for that Cowboy somewhere else. Don't waste your hopes on an imprint that is somehow Cowboy-averse, because that doesn't do anybody any good. Read those guidelines: learn them, live them, *love* them.

There is nothing shameful about writing to prompt. The prompt is there to ensure an expected response—one that will elicit feelings of intense emotion and joy.

You wouldn't give a cat to someone who's allergic to cats.

But know what you're doing—*love* what you're doing—and don't waste your acquiring angel's time by submitting something they don't want. Don't submit your 150,000-word masterpiece with multiple plot arcs and three different romantic leads to someone looking for a 55,000-word category romance. It's depressing for you and frustrating for your editor. Your masterpiece has another home— I'm sure of it. And your editor has lots of authors with strong voices and exciting new ideas waiting in line to write exactly the book she needs, and the one that readers expect.

CHAPTER 7:

NOPE TROPES—GIVING LOVE A BAD NAME

*Society has changed a lot in the last thirty years—
and category readers have been the first to demand
to see those changes in print. You can't feed social
backwardness to a category romance reader. They
know how the world has changed—and they expect
to see those changes reflected in the books they're
reading.*

Brenda Chin
Category Romance Editor

BEFORE I start this section, I'd like to make two things about myself clear.

I don't believe in calling authors out publicly. It's unprofessional, it's damaging, and it creates an environment of fear—a witch-hunting environment—in which people point at an author and scream, "SHE'S DONE WRONG!" to milk outrage for clickbait, and the unwitting targets who just want to do right are grievously bullied and misled. If you disagree with an author's subtext, her message, her prose choice, by all means have that conversation privately, if you feel comfortable doing so and can be civil about it. Otherwise, starting judgy kerfuffles in public is a good way to scare off your readership and damage your professional relationships.

I don't believe in shaming readers for their flavor of happy. Ever. You really *never* know what book, what trope, what tiny section of prose is going to save someone's life. I'll never forget going to dinner with some friends of my husband and having the wife offer a tentative conversation starter:

"Have you read XYZ?"

"Oh my God—no—those books are terrible. The prose is terrible, the characterization is terrible, the representation was terrible."

hurt silence "Oh, I'm sorry you feel that way. Those books saved my marriage."

"Uh… well, you know. They can't be *all* bad."

Never again will I put that look on someone's face. Ever. It's one of the most horribly insensitive things I've ever done, and I cringe when I remember the dogpiles I jumped on while doing the same thing online. A person's happy is a tentative, personal thing—shaming them away from the things that allow them, for however long, to escape the slings and arrows of what is often a difficult life is such an emotional violation. I'm ashamed of the times I bought into the idea that this was an okay thing to do.

Gentle education? Sure. But howling like the righteous Cerberus at the gates of genre? Unnecessary and unprofessional.

That being said, that doesn't mean there aren't some tropes in romance literature that are harmful and deserve extinction.

Please keep in mind that nobody writes a romance book thinking, "This is going to hurt my readers and that's fine with me!" Like any other form of entertainment or public discourse, as society and awareness evolve, so does our response to the way things were done at the beginning versus the way things are done now.

Remember old television shows in which there were advertisements for cigarettes and smoking was part of the dialogue? As a whole, we realized smoking was bad for us, and people didn't want their kids to see their actor idols doing it. The commercials were removed and on-screen smoking was phased out of the programming. We felt that it was better not to have something that caused cancer made to look sexy and acceptable.

True, the tropes we're talking about aren't as insidious as cancer. Let's move things up the timeline a little bit. I'm old enough to remember the old perfume commercials that featured women who could "bring home the bacon and fry it up in the pan, and never, ever, ever let you forget you're a man!" Those commercials were catchy at first—empowering. This woman could wear a business suit, an apron, and a negligee, all in the same evening! It wasn't until the seventies progressed into the eighties and nineties that we realized we were killing ourselves trying to cook, clean, raise the kids, and rule the universe all at the same time. And dammit, why couldn't someone else cook and clean, right?

And these gaffes and stereotypes get vilified as the world progresses. We forget that they once served a valuable purpose in changing the way we see ourselves for the better. Barbie, for instance, the much-maligned small-footed blond toy from Mattel. Yes, eventually it occurred to us that little girls could get a terrible self-image from this doll. If they didn't have wasp waists, legs to their chin, and blue eyes the size of doorknobs, they felt like they were failing at life. But before *that* realization, there was also the realization that girls could be doctors or veterinarians or surfers or athletes—just like Barbie. When the horrible self-image problems came to light, Barbie changed. Now there are dolls that my roundish freckled daughters with the red hair and the baby-bearing hips can identify with, as well as a number of different complexions and physio-types designed to make sure no little girl feels left out. Will this work? Well, I hope so—I sort of like the new Barbies, I'll be honest. But even if it doesn't and the toy has to change again, the point is, it *changed*.

So can romance.

MOLDY OLDIES

HERE ARE some tropes that started out as a bridge to change the way we thought of gender, relationships, and sexuality and that have now outlived their usefulness to become downright harmful. We don't need to shame the authors of these tropes, and we don't need to terrify readers into not reading them. We just need to be aware that they're out there and that they can be as damaging to readers' emotional health as the small-footed wasp-waisted blond or the woman who feels the need to do it all.

And we can help them evolve, one book at a time.

NO MEANS YES

What it is: This is one of the original romance tropes, in which an ingenue gets swept away by passion and seduced by an older, wiser man. While she says "no" with her words, she's saying "yes" with her body, clearly giving the hero permission to ravish her.

Why it was useful: Back in the 1930s when Mills & Boon first started focusing on escapist fiction for women, there were "good girls" and "bad girls," and the bad girls were busy out having great sex while the good girls were only reading about it. The good girls wanted to have the sex—they *longed* to have the sex—but they were good girls. Letting go and screaming, "Oh yes! Do that thing you're doing *right there! And to the left! And lower!*" was not in good girls' emotional makeup. It was really much easier for a "good girl" to dream about being swept away by passion with a man who could read her mind.

What has changed: Women are demanding sexual agency and recognize the language of sexual assault. When a man says, "Your mouth says no, but your body says yes," what he's really saying is, "You poor sweet child, you really don't know what's good for you, but *I* do." Only women aren't having any of that anymore. If she wants to get banged like a screen door in a hurricane, *there is nothing wrong with that*. She is allowed to have those needs and find a suitable partner who will help her meet them. Consent matters.

Why it is harmful now: It gives women—especially *young* women who are reading these books as sort of a blueprint for how relationships work—the idea that their words, their desires, don't matter… that men can force sex on them. It tells them that they might as well give in to unwanted advances, because even if they say no, no means yes.

Ways this trope has evolved: The idea of someone who is usually prim and proper and sexually closed-off letting loose is still a very attractive fantasy, but I think today we see this in more empowering ways. The hard-headed career woman who doesn't want entanglements looking for one night to blow off some steam is this generation's version of *No Means Yes*, and so is the Sexual Butterfly. There are ways for a character who has not been sexually adventurous to try new, exciting avenues without being pressured—or seduced— into doing so. We need to explore those tropes with more fervor and leave *No Means Yes* in the dust.

I Stalk You Because I Love You

What it is: This is the trope that features the super protective hero (or heroine, but it's usually a man) who stalks the object of his affection just to make sure nothing bad happens to them.

Why it was useful: This trope let single women—and men—feel protected. Even today, in the age of guard dogs, martial arts classes, and silent alarms, being alone can make a person feel vulnerable. And the idea of a guardian angel with your number really is a comfort.

Also, as a literary device, this trope did active duty. One thing it gave us was a reason for the hero to be right there to save the other main character when bad shit went down. "Oh my God! There's a loup-garou here to break my furniture and eat my cat! Thank God the hero was here to save me!" The other reason was to create conflict between the two main characters. "I'm not a child!" "I didn't say you were!" "But you're stalking me!" "I'm protecting you!" And if the guy just killed a loup-garou, there's not much argument there.

What has changed: Well, martial arts classes, guard dogs, silent alarms, and area awareness, for one. Nowadays, if a single person living alone feels threatened, they are not afraid to say so and to establish some form of self-protection. So we expect our heroes/ heroines to be more empowered, not necessarily needing to be saved from themselves, usually. But there's more than that.

"Stalking" somebody because you "love" them implies that you don't trust them enough to tell them you're out there. Even if there is a sudden loup-garou infestation in your neck of woods, why not invite your significant other over to your place, where you've set up loup- garou booby traps all over the perimeter and had a shaman cast a spell of loup-garou repellent over your threshold?

Why it is harmful: Loup-garous and tongue-in-cheek aside, stalking is a serious problem. Being watched without your permission is invasive and creepy. Having somebody with violent tendencies hanging out around your house without your permission is more likely to lead to domestic abuse than it is to catching a supernatural entity. It is important that we don't let anyone think their privacy is violable in the name of "love."

On a more personal note, I've never really censored what my children read. When my daughter—grown now—was in her teens, she was reading a very popular series that featured a character who "stalked" his girlfriend because she was sort of a klutz. One of my proudest moments was when my daughter drew a comic showing what she would do if some guy just showed up randomly saying, "I'm stalking you because I love you."

It featured her wielding a baseball bat and screaming for her father.

Because seriously, having some bozo pop up at her window and say, "'S'up. You awake?" would be terrifying. No kid should have to worry about that.

Ways this trope evolved: Communication and consent. We still like our protectors to protect, but we don't want them to overstep their boundaries. Instead of "I stalk you because I love you," our alpha protectors can offer to assign guards, they can offer to sleep on the couch, they can tell the threatened person they're going to swing by and watch the place. They can offer to call first, they can offer to improve home security. There are a whole lot of ways for a protector and the protected to be in forced contact that don't threaten the agency of the person being protected. And if there is no threat, arranging to bump into your crush in a public place and then being willing to take no for an answer can be a very positive way to further the relationship.

TOO STUPID TO LIVE (TSTL)

What it is: This usually involves a protagonist, often female, who cannot make the simplest decisions or take independent action. The idea is that one of the main characters is frequently in trouble and so obsessed with his or her own independence that, like a child going "Let me help get that ball in the street!", this character often puts themself in danger.

Where it came from: This is all conjecture on my part, but I think part of this trope originated from the oh-so-hilarious notion that people who step outside their gender roles are doomed to failure—sometimes because they try too hard. So if a woman wants to help her Protector/Law Enforcement foil with the investigation or protection, she is only bound to make things worse. If a man is forced to raise children, he will only end up feeding the baby chili and using the iron to cook grilled cheese *à la* Michael Keaton in *Mr. Mom*. (My husband adores that movie, by the way. I keep telling him that if I hadn't been able to trust him with our children, I wouldn't have married him in the first place.)

Another thing that contributes to this trope is the Fiercely Independent character trope. The idea here is that everybody needs *somebody*, and in this case, this fiercely independent person needs a Protector to protect them from themselves.

What has changed: Mostly, readers have gotten savvier—and have started demanding characters as smart as they are. Our readers are like a horror-movie audience. Nowadays, when the blond girl goes "Here, I'll walk into the basement all by myself because there's a serial killer here and we should split up!", we all throw popcorn at the screen. Romance readers are like, "Oh for sweet fuck's sake, woman, say, 'Not today, murder room, not today!' and walk away!" Smarter readers demand characters who make better decisions—and who act in their own best interests and in the best interests of their significant others. TSTL characters can read as authorial laziness; they create problems so a plot can emerge from thin air.

Why this trope is harmful: It's demeaning and implies that people can't think for themselves. Instead of driving the romance through legitimate human conflict, it drives the plot by random acts of fateful cockup, and that makes us all look bad. In this day and age, it's unlikely that anyone who can learn to use an iPhone is that dim about a real crisis.

Why sometimes we need it: Okay,   this   one's   from experience. In my urban fantasy series, I had a character who was drunk with grief and her own bravery rush into a really dangerous situation to save her beloved. About three years after the book came out, a reader said, "I loved that part, but why didn't she just do this, this, and this, and then that wouldn't have happened?" And I said, "That would have been a *great* idea. Next time you write the book because I'd love to read that!" Because sometimes what looks like a Too Stupid To Live protagonist is really an author who isn't a god and who would make the same mistake.

How it's evolved: Essentially the Too Stupid To Live protagonist has become the Trouble Magnet, and if you're wondering at the difference, it's in the agency. A Too Stupid To Live character creates trouble for themselves by making poor decisions based on lack of communication and hubris. A Trouble Magnet is a trouble magnet because they don't just let life happen to them, and every decision they make is something they take moral responsibility for. In my example of a Trouble Magnet, I talked about the friend who goes to the dry cleaner's, sees a robbery, feeds a homeless child, and comes home in Witness Protection as a foster parent. That's a character who is compassionate enough to care for a stranger and brave enough to stand up for what's right. The fact that the robbery went down at the dry cleaner's is not her fault—and maybe the character's choices made her life a little complicated, but she took responsibility for that.

'TIS A PITY SHE'S A HO-BAG

What it is: This is a trope in which a rapist (I mean, hero) goes out of his way to "have" someone (usually a woman) presumed to be sexually promiscuous. Then—usually right when she gives in—he finds out she's not that kind of girl and refuses to fuck her because she's a virgin and he doesn't do virgins; they're complicated.

Where it started: This is a variation of the Mistaken Identity or the Disguise tropes, in which the character is mistaken for somebody they're not. It dates back to the days when a woman's reputation as "pure" could make or break her marketabi—I mean, marriageability. This is a way for a man to be "seduced" by a woman's personality because even when he thinks she's a total whore who should just drop trou and bend over, there is "something about her" that flips his switch. When he finds out she's a virgin, he's at first repulsed and finally intrigued enough to marry her, so they can have pure sex.

What has changed: God, a lot, I hope. For starters, a person's worth is no longer judged by hymen or ignorance. For finishers, it *really* pisses readers off when a seducer assumes that just because someone's had other lovers, they should say, "Okay!" when propositioned by some asshole who doesn't want entanglements.

Why it's harmful: It's rapey, it's demeaning, it implies sexual history represents a source of shame or guilt, and it lets hedonists off the hook for having a one-night stand if they think whomever they're hooking up with is "loose." It also deprives a character who's had no sex of the agency to choose the person to have it with. If anyone wants to get busy with a hot alpha for a one-night stand, that's their business. And to say, "No, I'm not having sex with you because you're a virgin and that means we have to get married!" is insulting to the virgin's agency—and an experienced person's previous decisions.

How it has evolved: Well, first of all, even when they're assuming someone is a sexual powerhouse, the other MC still treats them with respect. Second of all, when our more experienced character finds out the other character is a virgin, our Jade puts the virgin off with "It should be special—and I'm not special enough for you." And then our virgin seduces the more experienced main character. And since the experienced main character thought the virgin was pretty amazing in the first place, this gives everybody agency and self-worth. It's a win-win! (My editor suggested we name this trope What a Virgin Wants. This is also win-win!)

Sometimes this also evolves into a different scenario that doesn't demean someone for having a sexual history.

Look, it's not that virgins aren't romantic. First times and first love are *always* good things in romance. It's that having a sexual past shouldn't make *anybody* the target of sexual harassment and subjugation. This trope is a dinosaur left over from the days when a woman's virginity added to her innate value. People have so much more to offer than their virginity.

GAY/KINK/SLUTTY FOR YOU

What it is: This trope is used exclusively in gay or erotic romance, and it deals with a character who is so platonically in love with a gay/kinky/polyamorous friend that they'll gladly "switch teams," "venture into kink," or host orgies to please a partner.

Where it started: While there is something terribly seductive about the idea that a love for someone is so strong that it can change your basic desires or sexual orientation, I don't think that's where this trope started. I'm pretty sure it started with a misunderstanding of bisexuality and kink in general. In order to explain how a husband or wife with three kids sues for divorce and ends up happy with someone of the same gender, with whom they now curate a really interesting basement, people assumed they just "went gay" or were "turned gay" by an overtly gay person who enacted mysterious wiles. It was somehow easier for readers—and people in general—to believe that someone was "turned" than to understand that the ability to be happy with either gender had existed in this person all along.

What has changed: For one thing, bisexuality is a much more prominent topic now, and bisexuals have not been silent. For another, the entire LGBTQ community has been vocal about nontraditional sexualities *not* being communicable or catching but an intrinsic part of a person's identity since birth. This change of perception has rendered Gay for You or Kinky for You particularly archaic.

Why it's harmful: Being LGBTQ or kinky or sexualized shouldn't be considered something you can turn on or off at will— that way lies the barbarism of the pray-the-gay-away camps and slut-shaming. Sexual orientation is *not* a choice, but sexual activity should be.

Why it's tough to get rid of: The problematic thing about this trope is that I only know a few authors who actually write it—and believe it. The real problem is that I know an awful lot of novels that have been falsely identified as Gay for You or Kinky for You. The majority of these books have very clear coding in the backstory and emotions of their characters that indicate the character was bisexual or ready for kink but unaware of their own leanings—until this one person made them realize that they've been missing something all along. For some people this is a reality—social conditioning was so strong that they didn't recognize their sexuality until they were *really* attracted to one particular person.

Some readers—specifically readers with no prior knowledge of LGBTQ+ issues, kink, or the community as a whole—don't recognize the coding and don't understand bisexuality or kink. They see the term Gay for You and think, "Oh yes! I love those books!" Only they're not aware that the implications are really dangerous for members of a community threatened by vengeful churches and vitriolic politicians.

What's a good alternative: The simple answer is Out for You. The person's bisexuality or kink is announced to the world when they choose to be with this person of the same sex or erotic interests. The attraction has always been there, but this is the person they love enough to make it public.

A note of caution: This is more of a *reader-identified* trope than a *writer-generated* one. One of the things that we've started doing is not relying on coding and implication but stating the bisexuality or kink overtly. Stakes are getting too high for subtlety. People who think someone can "change their orientation" for one person might not hesitate to try to *force* them to change it back.

PLACES TO TREAD CAREFULLY

FORBIDDEN FRUIT can turn poisonous *fast*.

The following is a list of tropes that have the potential to go very, very, *very* wrong. In today's romance, characters need agency, consent, and equality. If there is any hint of power imbalance or abuse, the romance will ring false and facile. Ignore the traps in these tropes and readers will call you out, just as publishers will give you a wide berth.

Are these tropes bad by default? No.

But tread carefully. Remember: agency, equality, consent— these are the absolutes in this literature. Romance readers shouldn't settle for anything less.

MY BULLY/MY BELOVED

What it is: When a high school monster or past abuser comes back very remorseful and turns over a new leaf.

Potential for harm: Bullies leave scars. Abusers are criminals. Unless this character can make true, visceral atonement, people who have been bullied are going to feel victimized by this villain getting off the hook easily.

MAY/DECEMBER

What it is: When one of the characters is significantly—twenty years or so—older than the other. Note: this does *not* mean a five-year age difference. That's more like May/June. This is old enough to affect the power dynamic between two characters, which is why it can be a problem.

Potential for harm: Age has its privileges—and its responsibilities. An older person usually has more power and influence than a younger person, and the potential for abuse is high, as is the potential for a young person to abuse an older lover's reputation. This needs to be handled deftly and with great sensitivity or readers are not going to be comfortable with these two people ending up together.

ABDUCTION/STOCKHOLM SYNDROME

What it is: When a relationship starts as a kidnapping. The trope inevitably runs that the abductee decides to follow the abductor out of free will.

Potential for harm: If someone holds a gun to your head and then says, "I was wrong. Fly, be free!", your judgment has the potential to be impaired beyond free will. The power has already been abused. A comeback from kidnapping to romance is not only unlikely, odds are great it's unhealthy. Unless you can give the abductee power from the start—or prove that the abductor was trying very hard to save the victim from something horrible—this trope is going to go very, very wrong.

HOW TO MARRY A ZILLIONAIRE

What it is: In which one of the main characters has more money than God and that is both their appeal, their virtue, and their personality.

Potential for harm: Being completely financially dependent on someone else can erode character agency. It's impossible to find equal footing if one character has no power and the other character is no more than a meal ticket. The potential for abuse on both sides is tremendous. Just like in real-life situations, when one character is the breadwinner, the character without the money needs to have oodles of agency, and the character with the money needs to have a whole lot of redeeming qualities and character for this to work.

FAUX-CEST

What it is: When the main characters are steprelations or related by someone's marriage but not by blood.

Potential for harm: For one, incest is instinctively squicky to most humans, so make sure their separation is *really* apparent. But for another, a younger almost-relative has very little power in a relationship and the potential for abuse is huge.

HOT FOR AUTHORITY

What it is: A cute college professor and a student find chemistry outside of class. Cleric meets parishioner after hours, à la *Thorn Birds*. A psychiatrist gets up close and personal with a client. A cop can't resist a witness.

Potential for harm: A teacher holds an enormous amount of power over a student. Even in college, where both partners are of the age of consent, a failing grade is no joke. A cleric, a psychiatrist, a police officer—all of them hold enough power over certain populations that the potential for abuse is terrifying. In real life, this sort of affair could hold disastrous consequences for both parties. Power imbalance should not be treated lightly. It's really best to "distance" an authority relationship. Maybe the student isn't in the teacher's class. Definitely do not give the officer a position of power over the potential lover. A cleric or psychiatrist can't counsel the romantic partner. Handle this trope with kid gloves, or this trope is going to backfire on you.

This isn't the end, and these aren't the only toxic traps in classic categories.

We are—hopefully!—ever evolving to a different awareness, one that will give our readers the most enjoyment but that will also give them a fantasy worth striving for. If a trope encourages behaviors in our children that we would rather not see develop, it's worth asking if maybe we should stop writing it and not encourage it to be read.

EVOLUTION IS SCARY AND GOOD

IT'S HARD to let go of old favorites.

I'm old enough to remember when some of these tropes were really popular—Faux-cest was one of my personal faves, as was No Means Yes—but times change. It's sort of like watching old movies. You can watch the movie and think, "Yes, I love this movie! But that part there is unacceptable" (e.g. every beloved John Hughes teen flick[1]). You can still enjoy the movie for what it was for you *then* without allowing the problematic parts to be acceptable *now*.

I know it's scary when what's acceptable can change as fast as a shitstorm on the internet. I know it's hard when social media—one of a modern writer's most effective marketing tools—can become a dumpster fire with one out-of-context quote.

Just remember what we're working for.

Yes, we're working to entertain people, to take them away from lives that are often harder than they should be, but we're also working to give the world models of what life *can* be. Sensual and consensual romances, partnerships forged in equality, buoyed by consent, and founded with agency from both parties. We want our children to grow up knowing that consent is sexy, sexuality is extraordinary, and that the gift of a relationship is available to everyone who is willing to work on themselves and with another in order to be happy.

---

1 For a fascinating look at the problematic sexual and racial politics of John Hughes and his output by someone with a front-row seat, check out Molly Ringwald's brilliant essay, "What About the Breakfast Club?" *The New Yorker* (April 6, 2018) (https://www.newyorker.com/culture/personal-history/what-about-the-breakfast-club-molly-ringwald-metoo-john-hughes-pretty-in-pink)

Changing the old tropes, the old ways, is hard. Looking at a world that thinks about sex, about gender, about life, differently than we did when we were young is hard.

But hopefully, ultimately, it's like the Happily Ever After in a good romance. Not easy, but damned satisfying when it happens. That is work that will save the world.

CHAPTER 8:

TREASURE—TAKING OUT THE TRASHY

The most useful thing for me as a writer was being told to always write the next book. On submission? Write the next book. Get rejected? Write the next book. Bad sales? Write the next book. Always move forward. Always keep writing.

Maisey Yates
The Librarian Talks
July 25, 2016

A ROMANCE WRITER'S WORK IS NEVER DONE

ONE OF the most excellent and seductive things about craft books is that there is constantly more to say. Category romances are considered a good place for romance writers to start, but I've always considered them an art form all their own. They are, in fact, a good place for romance writers to polish their skills, to understand the basics of their craft, to remember the purity of the romance drug and the high it brings readers in a perfectly legal burst of words.

But romance—like society, like literature, like audience expectations—is constantly evolving. I highly doubt this will be the final word on the art of category romance.

Nevertheless, I hope there are some valuable takeaways here. As you begin your category romance, keep the following things in mind:

Be cognizant of your tropes and their importance in fulfilling reader expectations.

Identify the kind of happy you're building for readers who crave it.

Start with characters and how they change as individuals and as a couple.

Structure your plot to have an internal and external conflict that keeps escalating.

Compress wherever possible—in character, conflict, plot, relationships, setting—so that each detail does multiple duties.

Allow the intimacy to build toward the life-changing climax.

Anchor your conflicts by tracing them to their sources and making those sources work overtime!

Beware of trope traps and outdated gender expectations.

Study and honor the guidelines as you navigate the submission process.

Find new and exciting ways to tell the oldest story in the world.

Find your own unique voice and let that speak in your story.

And finally, celebrate your work!

THE CELEBRATION OF ROMANCE

IT'S FUNNY... I can remember the first category romance I ever read, but I can't remember the time frame. I know this because Damon pressed me on it, and I couldn't figure out where that slim book fit between trying to check out Judy Blume's *Forever* and having the librarian call my father to ask for permission, and learning that the library let you check out category romances *without* telling your parents.

I just know that I owned that book. It was *mine*. I remember that because I read it again and again, until the spine fell apart and the pulp pages crumbled.

It was called *Solitaire* by Sara Craven. It is a classic Poor Virgin Nanny/Billionaire Rake book, and there is some making out, but the sex didn't happen until the end, off stage.

"In the time of every *jeune fille*, there is a time to lock the door. Your time is now."

And she did it. She locked the door and went back to her broody lover to get laid, get married, and be a stepmother to a really awful teenage boy.

I *loved* that moment.

When I started writing, I wanted there to be a breathless moment like that in every book I wrote. I don't know if I always succeed, but in that moment, in that book, I got my first glimpse of how powerful romance was. Sure, I saw couples all around me—parents, grandparents, friends of the family—but I wanted to see how they got to be couples.

That was a magic thing there, an awesome new beginning. And the simplicity of the book—every sentence gave me a wealth of screen time in my imagination. How did it *do* that?

I was a rabid fantasy/science fiction reader through high school, but in between wrist-breaking tomes that involved three pages of codices and dictionaries for new languages, I also managed the sweet, slim volumes of romances that ended predictably but always kept me turning pages.

In college I would sit with my doorstop of an English literature anthology in my lap and hold a tiny pulp fiction novel in front of it so nobody could accuse me of slacking—or slumming. After I had children, I frequently became that mother with the baby on her hip, trying to cook dinner and finish my romance book all at the same time.

Once, when Mate and I were going through a particularly rough patch financially, when he was still going to school and my teaching job was only part-time, we realized that though we'd managed Christmas for the (at the time) two children, we couldn't afford to buy presents for each other. The kids were *just* old enough to notice that type of thing.

Well, I had a pair of new jeans I'd bought for my husband, so I wrapped those up from Santa. And at that time, I got a happy little package once a month, with four red-bound volumes of delectable nonfattening brain candy that kept me sane, a little bite of fantasy at a time. I wrapped those up for myself. Those were my Christmas presents that year, and I didn't love the books any less because they came with pretty paper and a bow.

So as much as I loved romance—and, later, paranormal romance and urban fantasy—you'd think I'd have been proud to write it. But women's literature, their loves and lives, don't get a lot of respect from our society, and they certainly didn't twenty years ago.

When I started writing my first book—an offshoot of a master's program—my colleagues in the English department asked me what I was writing.

"Vampires," I said with a smile.

"Oh, like, horror?"

"No...."

"Oh, magical realism?"

"God, no."

"So like...."

"You know." And here it is. The kiss of death. "Trashy vampire romance."

"But why? You're so *smart*."

And my tongue bound up behind my teeth and I was back to being that thirteen-year-old pressed by her grandfather, smirking and shrugging, like heh, heh, it was all about the sex, right? Just for fun. Not a big deal. Right?

But I self-pubbed the book, and gave out copies, and one woman—a colleague's wife who worked in the Special Education department—adored it, and all the ones that followed.

One day I walked into the staff room and found a horror show. My department head had grabbed a copy of one of my books from my friend while Rebecca had been doing a reread, and Patrick was doing a mock dramatic reading of the first chapter out loud, to the entire staff room.

My friend was in tears, and the audience—all men—was jeering and hooting appreciatively.

"Yup, that's *trashy romance* all right!"

Rebecca and I looked at each other in agony. The book had meant something to *me* because I'd written it. But it had meant something to *her* because she loved it. Completely. With all her heart. It was like watching her child get shamed and being unable to speak up.

I stopped calling my books "trashy vampire romance" after that. That woman—*every reader*—who loves a story with all their soul deserves respect.

We live in a hard world. On any given day, even those of us who are well off can name five soul-crushing, dream-killing, I-can't-believe-the-world-works-like-this news events, possibly before coffee. If there is an art form that gives somebody hope to get through a day that *starts* like that?

That art form deserves to be praised to the skies.

One of the reasons Damon Suede and I love to yap at each other about the nature of a Happily Ever After over leisurely lunches is because, in our cores, we believe the one true thing about romance. Romance is the language of hope. It is not the language of the uneducated, the bored, or the terminally disappointed.

Where do those beliefs come from, anyway?

Damon's belief about the HEA stems from Aristotle's *Poetics*, one of Western literature's oldest documents about the rules of storytelling. It posits that comedy—a.k.a. romance—ends with a wedding or the birth of a child. *Hope*.

My belief about the HEA stems from the romances that Eleanor of Aquitaine imported from France to England, the legends of King Arthur that permeate our literary awareness, which state that the personal concerns of our characters—say, the tragic relationship of Arthur, Guinevere, and Lancelot—are just as important to an audience as the political machinations and the state of kings. And, if we remember, that ended *badly*. But it was important, because their personal lives were important, and they were searching for happiness. And that meant something to us.

Hope *matters*.

No matter who you side with, we are neither of us uneducated. Neither of us is bored or frustrated. *We love this art form*.

But we don't write stories about politics or the affairs of kings—unless it's a king of a tiny fictional country that nobody's heard of in search of the consort of his dreams.

Romance is not politics—although it *is* political. It is not tragedy. It is not *Macbeth, Othello, Hamlet*, or *King Lear*. But that doesn't mean it's not Shakespeare. Romance is *As You Like It*, *Twelfth Night*, and *The Merchant of Venice*.

Again—so why the bad rap? Is it the structure?

Anybody who has watched any action movie *ever* has enjoyed a formula—just not *this* one. We've been telling that story again and again for a couple thousand years. Horror, suspense, epic fantasy—for every genre there is a breakdown like the one I offered. Freytag's Pyramid does different, specific things in each genre. *There is a* structure *for every type of genre fiction.* And in every type of fiction, it's the power of the storytelling voice and the freshness of the story that makes the structure new and interesting and fun.

Maybe it's the Happily Ever After?

A century of mockery and disdain because romance offers us a hopeful future? Not for kings or countries but for individuals, people whose very existence is thwarted and hindered by the kings and countries who don't care for their citizens as individuals? Is it that kings and politicians and academics are so concerned with the grand affairs of state that a simple story about happy individuals is brushed off as a fairy tale, of no consequence and no quality?

Or is it that romance—the grand stories of the most singular characters—is generally perceived as a woman's genre?

Maybe the worry for civil rights and the care of the family and the happiness of each person in the family unit is designated as a feminine concern, and men really don't have time to make sure people in their world are happy, and so they write it off, out of hand.

If that's the case—and I do suspect that, with a few exceptions, it could be—then romance writers should not just be *proud* of their work, they should be *furious* that it is ever called into question. We are writing a brighter future.

Romance books are taken on planes to quiet nervous fliers, to hospitals to help comfort the sick or the grieving, or just to bed, to help calm the stress of the day. They're given as gifts to mothers who need to read something that wasn't made to teethe on, to grandmothers who love to remember their own first love, to single friends who are still poignantly hopeful that they'll get their own happily ever after. They're taken on vacations, saved for the beach, dangled at the end of a long week like a carrot on a stick.

I save my favorite books and my favorite authors for plane trips, because I get long stretches of uninterrupted reading time with the added bonus of a setup that lets me knit at the same time.

And while our readers often call our books guilty pleasures, housewife porn, or pulp fiction—often with a blush and a rather sheepish look because, *hey*, they're educated, they're intelligent, they're obviously capable of digesting political tomes and autobiographies—we all know the truth. Without that book, that Kindle special, that pulpwood paperback, that perfectly crafted literary truffle designed to go down like silk, they might not make it through the week without a good long cry.

And if they *do* make it, pulling themselves up by their bootstraps and forging bravely into a boring job, another week of housework, or a totally fulfilling life that sometimes feels like a hamster wheel of doom, they'll be a lot less refreshed, a lot less happy, a lot less *hopeful* than they will be if they get their romance fix.

Any devoted romance reader will tell you that reading a category romance gives readers the same racing heart, the same endorphin rush, the same little chemical zing in their system as chocolate or caffeine.

Imagine that—all the side effects of a mild stimulant with just words.

Just a Happily Ever After.

Just hope.

Romance writers, be proud of that treasure, be proud of what you do, be proud of your ambition to write, to be published, to write some more. Be proud of your *genre*, of what it represents, of what it can mean to people, to your readers, to the people who treasure every book, even if they feel like they have to hide the covers so the world doesn't crap on their happy.

When you do your job right, you have given someone a moment of joy—and that's such a pure thing. Remember back to your first romance book, your *Solitaire*, and remember that thrill of excitement when the main characters flirted, the way your heart pumped when they kissed, the flush of triumph when the book ended and you knew without a doubt that they would be happy forever after.

That's what you give people with your words.

That's what you're striving for when you pick up a book like this to help you do better.

What you want to write is worthy. Your genre is important and beautiful and amazing. And fun.

Don't forget to have fun.

Writing is hard enough—it really is—and full of self-doubt and agonizing decisions (they're, there, or their—augh!).

Don't agonize over romance. Celebrate it.

You're writing something wonderful.

You're going to do great things.

Appendix A:

Occupations and Hobbies

THE FOLLOWING is a *very incomplete* list of occupations that lend themselves to tropes, organized into categories for you to choose from. *Feel free to add to or expound upon* this list! It's meant as a starting point and nothing else.

Job Tropes

Business

Stock broker, IT, banker, financier, small business owner, café owner, bar owner, boutique owner (any flavor), accountant, office manager, HR director, security guard

Computers

Computer engineer, computer hacker, gamer, coding engineer, software engineer, lab technician

Entertainment

Television actor, screen actor, stage actor, backstage manager, prop manager, light and sound engineer, director, playwright, producer, novelist, biographer, singer, rock star, dancer (ballet, pop, jazz, tap, backup, diva, chorus), theme park actor, artist, caricaturist, animator, game designer, classical musician, rock musician, hip-hop musician, blues musician, clown, juggler, mime, circus performer, cruise director, travel agent, job agent, job manager, accountant

Health and Fitness

Fitness trainer, aerobics instructor, nutritionist, diet counselor

INTELLIGENCE COMMUNITY
CIA agent, covert ops military, spy

JOURNALISM
Investigative journalist, anchor, on-the-spot-reporter, blogger, corporate sponsor, network manager, film editor

LAW ENFORCEMENT
Policeman, detective, FBI, US Marshal, sheriff or deputy, PI, lawyer, prison guard

MEDICAL
Doctor, nurse, paramedic, lab tech, pharmacist, X-ray tech, physician's assistant, hospital administrator, Doctors Without Borders, researcher

MILITARY
Officer, enlisted man, Army, Navy, Air Force, Marines, Coast Guard

POLITICAL
Activists, lobbyists, politicians, aides, volunteers, Secret Service

SEARCH AND RESCUE
Firefighter, paramedic, EMT, dog handler, helicopter pilot, small plane pilot, mercenary adventurer, horse patrol

SPORTS
Football, basketball, hockey, golf, soccer, curling, ice skating, track and field, lacrosse, volleyball, swimming, water polo, anything else you can think of… players, managers, trainers, fans, and agents for all of the above

TEACHING
Teacher, coach, tutor, administrator, volunteer, professor, teacher's aide, bus driver, professor, college TA, college student

And so on. If you can think of a job and it has an instant set of expectations and understood behaviors attached to it, you have a romance trope to deal with.

HOBBY TROPES

This can include any amateur version of a career, period. The sky is the limit here. Here's a short list to get you thinking.

ANIMALS

Cats, dogs, fish, horses, pets of any sort, showing animals of any sort (can also qualify as a job)

ART

Crafting of any sort, crocheters, fiber artists, knitters, model making, movies, music, painting, photography, ranchers who care for fiber-making animals, sewing, spinners, theater/community theater, weavers

COLLECTING

Bugs, coins, dolls, shoes, stamps, weapons

FOOD AND DRINK

Baking, cocktails, gourmet culture, holiday baking and decoration

GAMING

Board games, RPGs, video games

LIFESTYLE

Antiques, bird-watching, clubbing and bar culture, gardening, fashion, people-watching, travel

MONEY

Gambling, investment

NEW AGE
Astrology, numerology, tarot and other divination

RESTORATION
Architecture, automobile, clothing, furniture

SCIENCE
Astronomy, programming, robotics, technology

SPORTS
Biking, caving, exercise, hiking, rock-climbing, sports-watching

VEHICLES
ATVs, boats, cars, hobby aircraft, motorcycles

VOLUNTEERING
Charity of all types, community service including volunteer versions of any entertainment or sports jobs, outreach programs, soup kitchens

Appendix B:

Narrative Tropes

The Big Misunderstanding

Two LOVERS are driven apart because one of them suspects the worst of the other. Sometimes there is a fight and wounded pride and rash decisions, or sometimes there is some dishonesty and subterfuge—just not the terrible betrayal suspected by the other lover.

Examples include: Friend's Betrayal, Imagined Betrayal, Mistaken Identity, Getting Dumped, the Wrong Ring, Other Twin, Communication Breakdown, Imagined Broken Promise.

Potential conflicts: Two people love each other but have problems communicating—or just believing the best of the person they love most. Big Misunderstanding taps into Background/Education. If you use this trope, make sure you are using it in a substantial way, something that has been foreshadowed and built into the character or plot. Misunderstandings that could be solved by a four-sentence conversation will irritate your readers. Make certain major confusion is justified and credible, because this trope can veer all too easily into Too Stupid To Live territory and audiences will punish you for that.

The Big Secret

One character keeps something huge and life-changing from the other character for any one of a number of reasons. This trope usually requires the two characters to learn to trust each other, as well as various levels of forgiveness and acceptance.

Examples include: Secret Baby, Lost Letters, Disguise, Masquerade, Secret Identity, Mistaken Identity, Fake Relationship/ Engagement, Love Triangle.

Potential conflicts: Holding on to a secret provides lots of internal conflict, especially when intimacy makes somebody want to confess. It also provides for external conflict as one lover struggles to cover up the signs of something not quite right. Big Secret taps into a conflict of Agendas in a big way. Remember that not all characters learn the truth or understand the lie at the same time. Context is critical! Weigh the emotional impact of giving and withholding the vital information.

ENEMIES TO LOVERS

The main characters are either in opposing camps via the institutions they represent—prosecuting attorney vs. defense attorney, doctor vs. nurse—or they really don't like each other. Their personal interactions need to be tinged with respect for an opponent and attraction to someone who really turns their key.

Examples include: Blackmail, Opposites Attract, Forced Cooperation, Forced Contact, Class Warfare, Office Enemies, Homecoming, Revenge, More Alike than Different, Lover in Peril, Suspicious Minds, Big Secret, Romeo & Juliet.

Potential conflicts: So wrong, but so right! There are a *lot* of potential sources for conflicts here. Conflicting Agendas, Philosophies, Education, and Background—*something important* had to drive that central opposition, which means their love needs to be big enough to overcome it. Provide intense, authentic barriers, and then force them to grow past them for maximum character building.

FAIRY-TALE RETELLING

Classic fairy-tale elements appear in the story—although the retelling doesn't have to follow the original beat for beat.

Examples include: Cinderella, Beauty and the Beast, Snow White and the Seven Totally Platonic Roommates, Twelve Wild Ducks, Snow White and Rose Red, pretty much any beloved folktale.

Potential conflicts: The conflict in the retelling can be the same as in the original—or updating the story to the present can also update the conflict. For example, in "Cinderella," the original conflict was mostly between Cinderella and her stepmother and sisters. In the recent film and novel updates, the conflict has become about Education and Background, as well as Philosophies and Agendas. There are lots of ways to exploit the conflict of the old story and new expectations—you're not locked in to the original plot or character conflicts in any way, shape, or form. Going against the fairy-tale grain can reveal surprising complexity and texture in beloved characters.

FANTASY/WISH FULFILLMENT

These tropes are exactly what they claim to be—that all-important wish fulfillment, the "If I could have any romance, I would have *this*." Going back in time, being a prince/princess, suddenly having a rich family, finding a soul mate, being able to succeed in a field or situation that you actually have no training for—the list goes on.

Examples include: Time Travel, Royalty, Lost Heir, Soul Mate/ Fated Lover, Lover Where Art Thou, Instant Baby, Instant Family, Overnight Celebrity, Fish Out of Water, Lover in Peril.

Potential conflicts: Well, all of them, mostly. It depends on the fantasy.

FIRST LOVE

The very first love affair—so many conflicts. Also, so many ways for it to go wrong. These days, unless the First Love story is a New Adult book, most First Love books are about rekindling that romance after it broke up. Still, many of these examples are good in flashback, and the First Love trope can also be used in conjunction with tropes like the Big Misunderstanding and the Big Secret.

Examples include: Losing the V-card, Too Young/Stupid/ Stubborn, *Somebody* Doesn't Approve, Return to Hometown, Love Triangle.

Potential conflicts: Everything. New lovers are bad at communication, worse at decision-making, and often are so busy finding themselves that they lose the person they're in love with. Add in any source of conflict with this plot trope and you will see fireworks. I should note that this trope is often done in retrospect, in conjunction with a reunion plot or even an Enemies to Lovers plot. The contrast between the passionate young lovers of the past and their cautious contemporary counterparts creates a lot of friction on its own.

FLING

The romance is not expected to last but does. There are a lot of moments in a person's life when they're not looking for a permanent relationship, and that's when these two people meet.

Examples include: Holiday Romance, One-Night-Stand-Who-Stayed, Amnesia, Cruise/Ski-Night Stand, Accidental Pregnancy, Fake Engagement, Jilted at the Altar, Runaway Bride/Groom.

Potential conflicts: This capitalizes on the sources of conflict found in people's Agendas and their Timing/Plans. Also, because some people tend to "hook up" with people we think are totally unsuitable for us, because, hey, it's only for a weekend or so, Background/Education and Philosophies can also be pretty ripe with conflict.

FRIENDS TO LOVERS

People who have known each other in a platonic sense suddenly see each other in hot new ways.

Examples include: Childhood Friends to Adult Lovers, Childhood Crushes/Adult Platonic Friends, In Love Since Puberty, Sympathetic Shoulder, Not Quite Related, Office Romance, Unrequited Love, Widow, Common Cause.

Potential for conflict: This one is big in the Preconceived Notions area. There was a reason these people weren't lovers to start with, and changing that reason is going to be a big deal.

FORBIDDEN LOVE

There are lots of reasons two lovers may feel as though they're star-crossed. Some are social, some are familial, and some are just self-perception. The point is, the romance slowly develops in a pressure cooker—not only must the lovers find out how they fit, but the world around them must too. The rough thing about this one is that some of these are trope traps—or, at the very least, must be treated carefully in order to give both characters complete consent, equality, and agency.

Examples include: Secret Romance, Family Feud, Secret Kink, Stepsiblings, Almost Kin, May/December, Polyamory, Dubious Consent, Hidden Engagement, the Worst Option, My Lover/My Kidnapper, Love Triangle, Romeo and Juliet, Best Friend's Sibling,

Best Friend's SO, Sibling's SO, Good Friend's *Adult* Child, Cougar/ Sugar Daddy, Cyrano, Guardian/Ward, Matchmaker Matched, Employer/Employee, Class Difference, Political Scandal, Widow, Childcare Worker.

Potential conflicts: The potential for conflict depends on why the love is forbidden but usually falls under Timing/Plans, Agenda, and Communication. Obviously this trope drastically amplifies the potential for intensity, eroticism, and angst. It's hard for lovers to get together under the best of circumstances. When the world around them wants them apart, that can get in the way. Sometimes Forbidden Love is actually the First Love, and this trope is brought up in retrospect during a Reunion. It's fun how these can all work together!

FORCED CONTACT

A plot device throws our lovers—possibly Enemies, possibly strangers, possibly exes—into contact more than they're comfortable with. Sometimes the contact is forced because of a ruse devised by one of the MCs to solve a problem, as in Fake Engagement, and sometimes it's something more pressing, as in two people who don't get along who have the same Agenda or mission. Either way, you can find Forced Contact in *many* different romance scenarios. The point is to put the lovers in a situation where they *must* talk to each other, be vulnerable together, be intimate, and where they can't just walk away if things get too difficult.

Examples include: Arranged Marriage, Accidental Pregnancy, Fake Engagement, Kidnapped, Marriage of Convenience, Matchmaker, Mail Order Spouse, Almost Kin, Protector/Bodyguard, Road Trip, Stranded, Suddenly Baby, Amnesia, Childcare Worker, Solve a Mystery, Find/Stop a Criminal.

Potential conflicts: Myriad. The one area in which the lovers usually do *not* conflict—particularly in a shorter novel where you have less time to unravel threads—is Agendas. Their Agenda is to stay together, no matter how much they want to throttle each other or run screaming to the opposite ends of the earth. Can their Agendas conflict? Sure. But that means paring down the other sources of conflict, especially in short form. Just remember, something's got to give in the interest of time, space, and common ground. If this is a mystery/suspense category, Forced Contact can give you a lot of personal conflict compressed with your plot conflict, and double duty is good!

HURT/COMFORT

This is the ultimate brave little soldier trope. One or both of the characters has been hurt in some way—damaged emotionally or physically or both—and the other protagonist provides the comfort and the impetus to recover. This trope can be particularly complex if both MCs have wounds, and part of the joy of this is to see how each protagonist's strength helps bandage the wounded parts in the other. It's the epitome of You Complete Me because the MCs are both so damaged in the beginning, but by the end they're a whole functioning entity.

Examples include: Wounded Warrior, Medical Care, Amnesia, Beauty and the Beast, Differently Abled, Pain is Gain, Trauma Survivor, Widow, and almost anything that happens in Painful Past.

Potential conflicts: Almost everything here has the potential for conflict—but Agendas and Philosophies are the big ones. One of these people has the agenda of "Leave me alone to soldier on!" and the other one has the agenda of "Fuck that! Get a grip and let me help you!" It's like fireworks with a dash of pain for spice.

PAINFUL PAST

This trope is much like Hurt/Comfort, with the caveat that one or both of the MCs has buried the source of their hurt deep in their hearts and getting them to talk about it is like pulling teeth. These two tropes can be very seductive and popular because baring your soul and allowing someone to help you recover creates almost instant intimacy. However, it's important to remember that abuse, assault, and PTSD are real problems with devastating impacts. Do your homework. Please remember not to exploit other people's pain. Be sensitive regarding the traumas you inflict on your characters—and be prepared for a book based on something truly traumatic to exceed your category length and turn into something else. This is why some books are longer than 50-60K.

Examples include: Scars, Return to Hometown, Intense Regrets, Wrong Regrets, Ho with a Heart of Gold, Redemption, Orphan, Widow, Grief Grappling.

Potential conflicts: Are everywhere, but again, Agendas are going to be a big one because one character almost always wants to stay silent and alone while the other wants to get to the heart of the grief—and this brings up Communication, and hello, isn't that always the way. These tropes—Hurt/Comfort and Painful Past are so prevalent, they are practically their own subgenre. Do be careful that you don't inflict anything on your characters that they cannot recover from—and that you are cognizant of the very human consequences of damaged people. You cannot hurt a character beyond agency.

REUNITED LOVERS

This trope is great for category romance because one of the hardest things to compress is the timeline of fitting a whole romance into such a short space. In this trope, the romance has already happened, but the lovers were parted. Sometimes it's external sources—new job, new school, etc.—but usually something else got in the way. It could be because of a Big Misunderstanding or a Big Secret, or it could just be because their sources of conflict—particularly Communication—overwhelmed their love. In any case, the sparks are already flying with this one. What remains is to let them ignite to flame.

Examples include: Second Chance, Working Together, Big Misunderstanding, Secret Baby, Forget the Fling, Big Secret, Lover in Peril, Homecoming, Love Triangle, Divorce Interruptus.

Potential conflicts: All of them, of course, but primarily Communication. What needs to happen with this trope is that the lovers have missed each other enough to have rearranged their Agendas or Philosophies, or improved upon their Education, or simply readjusted their priorities enough to make it work this time around. Notice how much this trope allows you to explore a character's past as well as their path to maturity and that HEA.

STRONG PROTAGONIST

Since the big climax in a romance is the fulfillment of intimacy, romancing somebody with emotional and physical strength into laying themselves bare is sort of a giant quest for the multiple Big O in emotional vulnerability. The Strong Protagonist is usually so used to being in charge that allowing somebody inside their defenses is a Herculean task, and the internal conflict is off the charts.

Examples include: Alpha/Badass, Billionaire, Sassy/Bossypants, Heir, Law Enforcement/Military, Cowboys, Vigilantes, Bodyguard/ Protector, Widow, Trauma Survivor.

Potential conflicts: A lot of internal conflicts in this one, a lot of clashing over Philosophies, Communication, and often Background/ Education. This is classic angst-bait to boot, so take full advantage of all that musky emotion. For a short-form romance, one of your people must be a better communicator than the other—you just don't have time to make them both brick walls. The payoff here is huge, but our Strong Protagonist needs to keep their basic personality structure in spite of character growth to encompass their significant other.

TICKING CLOCK

This trope gives a deadline to our lovers. Whether it's a deadline by which they can get together or one that ends their time together, it's a ticking clock in the background that not only gives the story a sense of urgency but also helps to give us a compressed timeline—and a reason for two complete strangers to fall in love in a week.

Examples include: Holiday Fling, Travel Transformations, Arranged Marriage, Forced Contact, Fake Relationship, One-Night Stand, Time Travel, Big Illness, Last Fling, Bachelor(ette) Party Favor.

Potential conflicts: This gives our lovers an adversary to fight and a reason to hash out all of their other conflicts, both internal and external. Racing the clock isn't just for suspense and bombs— knowing that unless our two MCs change themselves and their lives to accommodate the other, it gives them something to fight besides each other, and a reason to fight hard.

TIME FOR A CHANGE

This trope involves a protagonist who badly wants to change their stars, their self-image, their life. Of course, part of this trope involves self-improvement and character arc, but part of it involves seeing the good things that were inside this character to begin with. It also takes a complementary MC who sees all the good—and who respects the change as well.

Examples include: Stuck in a Rut, Fish Out of Water, New Horizons, Travel Transformation, Back to School, Top-Secret Recruit, Learning the Ropes, New Job/School/Town/Look/Skills.

Potential conflicts: So much to mine here, both internal and external. If the character changing has known the other MC for life, you have a Sexual Butterfly trope all ready to happen, and that is a conflict of Preconceived Expectations in a big way. If the character changing is in a new situation, you have everything from Preconceived Expectations, to Hierarchies, to Agendas, to Philosophies. Changing your own life is not easy, and changing it to accommodate another personality can make for a very challenging story. This encompasses everything from starting a new workout regime, to moving to a new town to start a new job, to going on a trip and assuming a false identity. The sky is the limit if you're breaking out of your everyday, and so is the potential for conflict here.

Appendix C:

The Exercises in Brief

Visualize Happy

In two or three words, how does your imaginary book make you feel?

What flavor do you want your happy to be?

Where and when might you find that flavor in the world?

Which characters offer you that happy?

Which adventures give you that happy?

PEEL BACK THE FOIL

List the things the characters have in common and the ways they are different.

WHAT DO THE CHARACTERS HAVE IN COMMON?	HOW ARE THE CHARACTERS DIFFERENT?

Then sum up with one statement each:

Main Character 1's agenda is....

Main Character 2's agenda is...

Both of them want to...

CHARACTERS	AGENDA
Character 1 wants…	
Character 2 wants…	
Both of them want…	

THE GRAMMAR OF CHARACTERS SPEAKING

THE AGENDA drives the character and makes them who they are. Almost everything you need to know can be derived from *what drives this character*.

Once you've decided what drives them, summarize them in a single, unforgettable sentence. This character must continue to deliver to that expectation for the *entire book*.

This sentence is a carefully chosen array of the words you feel showcase your character's most salient features, wedded together by a verb like *wants*, *needs*, *tries*, *must*, *can't*, or *demands*. In short, a verb that announces motivation.

ADJECTIVE + ADJECTIVE + NOUN PHRASE + WANTS + VERB PHRASE

_____+_____+_____+
WANTS +_____.

THE ADJECTIVE + NOUN PHRASE + ADVERB PHRASE + WANTS + VERB PHRASE

The_____+_____+_____+ WANTS
+_____.

NAME + APPOSITIVE + WANTS + VERB PHRASE

_____+_____+ WANTS +_____.

NAME + IS + NOUN PHRASE + WHO WANTS + VERB PHRASE

_____+ IS +_____+ WHO WANTS +_____.

TROPETASTIC CHARACTER MATH

What is your main character's trope? Take their motivation statement into account.

Who are they and what are they missing? What do they need in their life?

What "other" does your character's trope suggest? Example: the Jaded Heart trope suggests a young and chipper Boy or Girl Next Door.

Choose likely professions or occupations for the characters. (See Appendix A.) Don't forget that if you have a Mistaken Identity, their profession might not suit.

What are these characters' sources of conflict? Example: Hierarchy, Agenda.

What does the "other" need that the first character can give them?

What makes your characters people? Personality, dialogue, appearance, etc.

What are your characters' similarities? How are they different?
Similarities:

Differences:

What *specific* conflicts arise between these characters as a result of their sources of conflict? Example: Hierarchy—a sheriff and an FBI agent argue over jurisdiction.

Look at your characterizations and your tropes. What *doesn't* fit? What can you combine or compress? Cross out details you don't need.

MAPPING CHARACTER CONFLICTS

Look at the characters and character tropes. Where do their sources of conflict intersect and create the friction that can drive the plot? What common ground can save the relationship? Remember to compress—occupation can serve the character trope, and character trope can add to plot trope, and things can work together to drive the same conflict in fewer words.

SOURCE	CONFLICT	COMMON GROUND
Agenda		
Background/ Education		
Communication		
Hierarchy/Power Balance		
Philosophy		
Preconceptions		
Timing/Plans		

MOMENT MODELING EXERCISE A

Think of your favorite story and pick your favorite character trope and favorite plot trope from it.

Put those tropes in conjunction with other tropes to make an entirely different creature.

Keep that feeling that your favorite tropes gave you while creating your own original work.

ORIGINAL TROPE	DETAILS	KEEP OR CHANGE?	RESULTING TROPE CHANGES

MOMENT MODELING EXERCISE B

Pick a single trope—be it plot or character—from a favorite story and then build around it.

Change the environment, age, occupations, plot device, etc.

See if the story evolves into a different, complementary trope.

Appendix D:
Some Casual Recs

Everybody has a favorite romance—and one person's favorite isn't everybody's. I got this list through crowdsourcing (Twitter, Facebook) and word of mouth (thank you, Brenda Chin, LaQuette, and Cindy Dees!), looking for books that knew how to stroke popular tropes.

In most cases, you can spot the tropes used without any problem at all; that's the point! Some of these books are quite old. There are Nope Tropes here that will curl your hair, but they'll also show you what to beware of as you're writing, and that's good too. The variety is delightful. I found an entire series of Billionaires with different plot tropes, and an entire series of SEALS with the trope of Sexual Butterfly plain as day—and I'm sure with some looking around, you could spot those books too. In fact, anybody looking for a book that fell into their sweet spot could eyeball the book blurbs and know what was in store. It is like looking for the wrapper of your favorite candy bar—and just as wonderfully sweet.

This list *by no means* covers the entire list of tropes I've included in this book—which is only a partial taste of what's out there—but it's a place to start. Look at a few books, look at their blurbs, think about how you'd blurb the book *you* want to write. Which tropes would you announce, brazen and comfortable as red satin panties, on the cover of your beloved volume of romance?

Write what you love to read—tell the story nobody has written for you yet. But first identify exactly what you love to read and what story you want to tell. That starts with reading a book, and this is a place to look for exactly that.

Enjoy!

AUTHOR	TITLE	TROPES
Blake, Brynley	*Rogue*	Sexual Butterfly, Tragic Past, Big Secret
Blake, Brynley	*Renegade*	Sexual Butterfly, Friends to Lovers
Blake, Brynley	*Resurgent*	Sexual Butterfly, Friends to Lovers, Amnesia
Bond, Stephanie	*Club Cupid*	Friends to Lovers, Fantasy/Wish Fulfillment
Bourne, Phyllis	*Between a Rock and a Hot Mess*	Sexual Butterfly
Brockmann, Suzanne	*Prince Joe*	Disguise, Fish Out of Water, Forced Contact
Brockmann, Suzanne	*Letters to Kelly*	First Love, Tragic Past, Second Chance at Love, Wounded Warrior
Burchell, Mary	*Except My Love*	Forced Contact, the Big Secret
Calmes, Mary	*Lay it Down*	Wrong Twin
Carson, Caro	*The Colonels' Texas Promise*	Military, Friends To Lovers, Marriage Of Convenience, Single Parent, Second Chance, Damaged Goods
Craven, Sara	*Solitaire*	Virgin/Rake

AUTHOR	TITLE	TROPES
Daly, Barbara	*When the Lights Go Out...*	Mistaken Identity
Estrada, Rita Clay	*The Ivory Key*	Time Travel, Wish Fulfillment
Fielding, Kim	*A Full Plate*	Opposites Attract, Forced Contact, Big Secret, Roommates
Gates, Olivia	*The Desert Lord's Baby*	Big Misunderstanding, Secret Baby, Forced Contact
Gates, Olivia	*Temporarily His Princess*	Big Misunderstanding, Arranged Marriage, Forced Contact
Hauf, Michele	*Enchanted by the Wolf*	Arranged Marriage, Alpha Male
Jackson, Brenda	*Riding the Storm*	Virgin/Rake
Jackson, Brenda	*Taming Clint Westmoreland*	Sexual Butterfly, Fake Marriage, Forced Contact
Kelly, Dorien	*The Girl Most Likely To...*	Fling, Hidden Feelings
Kelly, Leslie	*Two to Tangle*	Wrong Twin, Fling, Big Misunderstanding, (Mistaken) Workplace Romance
Korbel, Kathleen	*A Rose for Maggie*	Single Parent

AUTHOR	TITLE	TROPES
Kyle, Regina	*Triple Dare*	Return to Hometown, Strong Heroine
Kyle, Regina	*Triple Threat*	First Love, Tragic Past
Lamb, Charlotte	*Guilty Love*	Forbidden Fruit, Tragic Past
Lowell, Elizabeth	*Valley of the Sun*	Wandering Spirit, Home Sweet Home
MacAllister, Heather	*Bride Overboard*	Runaway Bride, Fantasy/Wish Fulfillment
McBride, Mary	*Darling Jack*	Fake Marriage, Forced Contact, Tragic Past
Mortimer, Carole	*The Devil's Price*	Big Secret, Second Chance at Love
Nelson, Rhonda	*The Player*	Protector, Big Secret
Phillips, Carly	*Simply Sensual*	Secret Agenda, Hero in Disguise, Protector
Rai, Alisha	*Hate to Want You*	Romeo and Juliet, Tragic Past, Forbidden Fruit
Rai, Alisha	*Hurts to Love You*	Romeo and Juliet, Forbidden Fruit, Big Brother's Bestie

AUTHOR	TITLE	TROPES
Reisz, Tiffany	*Her Halloween Treat*	Fling, Best Friend's Little Sister, Homecoming, Member of the Wedding, Secret Crush, Forbidden Attraction, Forced Contact
Rochon, Farrah	*I'll Catch You*	Sports Hero, Jaded Heart, Forbidden Fruit
Rochon, Farrah	*Field of Pleasure*	Tragic Past, Reformed Rake
Shroeder, Shannyn	*One Night with a Millionaire*	Fling, Instant Family, Jaded Heart
Sinclair, Dani	*The Man She Married*	Amnesia, Surprise Family
Stewart, Anna J.	*Always the Hero*	Wounded Warrior, Instant Family, Protector
Thompson, Vicki Lewis	*Pure Temptation*	Sexual Butterfly, Friends to Lovers
Thompson, Vicki Lewis	*My Nerdy Valentine*	Disguise, Forced Contact, Protector
Weber, Tawny	*A SEAL's Seduction*	Sexual Butterfly, Forbidden Fruit
Yaye, Pamela	*Seduced by the Tycoon at Christmas*	Big Secret, Holiday, Fling
Yaye, Pamela	*Seduced by the CEO*	Single Parent, Forbidden Fruit, Employer/Employee

AUTHOR	TITLE	TROPES
Yaye, Pamela	*Seduced by the Playboy*	Big Secret, Reformed Rake, Sexual Butterfly, Sports/Athlete
Yaye, Pamela	*Seduced by the Heir*	Big Secret, Second Chance at Love

AMY LANE lives in a crumbling crapmansion with a couple of growing children, a passel of furbabies, and a bemused spouse. She's been a finalist in the RITAs™ twice, has won honorable mention for an Indiefab, and has a couple of Rainbow Awards to her name. She also has too damned much yarn, a penchant for action-adventure movies, and a need to know that somewhere in all the pain is a story of Wuv, Twu Wuv, which she continues to believe in to this day! She writes fantasy, urban fantasy, and gay romance—and if you accidentally make eye contact, she'll bore you to tears with why those three genres go together. She'll also tell you that sacrifices, large and small, are worth the urge to write.

Amy is the author of almost 100 titles, including the RITA-nominated category romance *A Fool and His Manny*. Her award-winning fiction spans genres from contemporary romance (*Beneath the Stain*, *Bonfires*) and romantic suspense (the Fish Out of Water series) to urban fantasy (the Little Goddess series).

Website: www.greenshill.com
Blog:www.writerslane.blogspot.com
Email: amylane@greenshill.com
Facebook:www.facebook.com/amy.lane.167
Twitter: @amymaclane

THANK YOU so much for purchasing and using *Crafting Category Romance*. I hope you've found it practical and useful to your writing process. As a working author, you know how important word of mouth can be to a title's success. When you have a moment, please leave a good word for this book online, mentioning whatever specifics you found helpful, so writers who might benefit can see what helped you and why.